P9-DII-283

THE
HARVARD MEDICAL
SCHOOL GUIDE TO
ACHIEVING OPTIMAL

MEMORY

Other books from Harvard Medical School and McGraw-Hill

Living Through Breast Cancer by Carolyn M. Kaelin, M.D., M.P.H., with Francesca Coltrera

Beating Diabetes by David M. Nathan, M.D., and Linda M. Delahanty, Ph.D.

Eat, Play, and Be Healthy by W. Allan Walker, M.D., with Courtney Humphries

Healing Your Sinuses by Ralph B. Metson, M.D., with Steven Mardon

Lowering Your Cholesterol by Mason W. Freeman, M.D., with Christine Junge

Overcoming Thyroid Problems by Jeffrey R. Garber, M.D., with Sandra Sardella White

Monthly newsletters from Harvard Medical School

Harvard Health Letter
Harvard Women's Health Watch
Harvard Men's Health Watch
Harvard Heart Letter
Harvard Mental Health Letter

For more information, please visit us at
www.health.harvard.edu

JUL 2005

THE
HARVARD MEDICAL
SCHOOL GUIDE TO
ACHIEVING OPTIMAL

MEMORY

AARON P. NELSON, Ph.D.

HARVARD MEDICAL SCHOOL, BRIGHAM AND WOMEN'S HOSPITAL

WITH SUSAN GILBERT

McGraw·Hill

New York   Chicago   San Francisco   Lisbon   London   Madrid   Mexico City
Milan   New Delhi   San Juan   Seoul   Singapore   Sydney   Toronto

NORTHPORT PUBLIC LIBRARY
NORTHPORT, NEW YORK

*The **McGraw·Hill** Companies*

Library of Congress Cataloging-in-Publication Data

Nelson, Aaron.
    The Harvard Medical School guide to achieving optimal memory / by Aaron P. Nelson
with Susan Gilbert.—1st ed.
        p.   cm.
    ISBN 0-07-144470-X
    1. Memory.   2. Mnemonics.   I. Gilbert, Susan, 1950–   II. Title.

QP406.N456   2005
612.8′2—dc22   2005000878

Copyright © 2005 by the President and Fellows of Harvard College. All rights reserved. Printed in the United States of America. Except as permitted under the United States Copyright Act of 1976, no part of this publication may be reproduced or distributed in any form or by any means, or stored in a database or retrieval system, without the prior written permission of the publisher.

2 3 4 5 6 7 8 9 0   DOC/DOC   0 9 8 7 6 5

ISBN 0-07-144470-X

Interior design by Think Design Group, LLC
Illustrations on page 15 by Michael Linkinhoker, page 20 by Joanne Muller, page 25 by Harriet Greenfield

McGraw-Hill books are available at special quantity discounts to use as premiums and sales promotions, or for use in corporate training programs. For more information, please write to the Director of Special Sales, Professional Publishing, McGraw-Hill, Two Penn Plaza, New York, NY 10121-2298. Or contact your local bookstore.

The information contained in this book is intended to provide helpful and informative material on the subject addressed. It is not intended to serve as a replacement for professional medical advice. Any use of the information in this book is at the reader's discretion. The author, publisher, and the President and Fellows of Harvard College specifically disclaim any and all liability arising directly or indirectly from the use or application of any information contained in this book. A health care professional should be consulted regarding your specific situation.

This book is printed on acid-free paper.

For Margaret, Julia, and Ava

The true beloveds of this world are in their lover's eyes lilacs opening, ship lights, school bells, a landscape, remembered conversations, friends, a child's Sunday, lost voices, one's favorite suit, autumn and all seasons, memory, yes, it being the earth and water of existence, memory.

—Truman Capote

Contents

CHAPTER 5   55

Causes of Memory Problems

CHAPTER 6   95

When to See a Doctor

Acknowledgments

It wasn't long ago that the idea of treating people with age-related memory loss or devastating memory-robbing disease was considered akin to tilting at windmills. Much has changed over the past twenty years. I have the great fortune to practice at a time when (and in a place where) each day seems to bring us closer to unraveling the secrets of the brain and the mystery of human memory. We are on the brink of disease-modifying therapy and possess the potential to enhance normal cognitive function.

Writing a book is a group project. I am indebted to many people who have contributed to this work. Dr. Martin Samuels, Chairman of Neurology at Brigham and Women's Hospital, was instrumental in the sequence of events that put me together with Dr. Tony Komaroff, Editor-in-Chief at Harvard Health Publications. I am grateful for their confidence in supporting me in this project. Dr. Samuels also had the vision to create a space for behavioral neurology at the Brigham at a time when starting new clinical care units was a tough sell. Dr. Jonathan Borus, Chairman of Psychiatry at the Brigham, has been the other pillar of our division and an unflagging advocate for the work we do at the hospital and the medical school.

Editors Judith McCarthy at McGraw-Hill and Dr. Tony Komaroff at Harvard Health Publications have provided insightful guidance from the inception of this project. At Harvard Health Publications, Nancy Ferrari has been a compassionate overseer and Raquel Schott contributed strong work in bringing together the art and figures. Julia Anderson Bauer at McGraw-

Hill smoothly shepherded the book through the final stages of review and into production. Dr. Daniel Schacter at Harvard University generously gave permission to borrow from his wonderful work. Dr. Charles Guttmann in the Surgical Planning Lab at Brigham and Women's Hospital and Dr. David Snowdon and his colleagues at the nun study at University of Kentucky provided brain images to illustrate key points.

I feel privileged to work among a fabulous group of talented and thoughtful colleagues at Harvard Medical School and in the Division of Cognitive and Behavioral Neurology at the Brigham. Dr. Kirk Daffner has ably guided our group through the frequently stormy seas of academic medicine, with unstinting commitment to our triune mission of research, teaching, and providing cutting-edge clinical care for our patients. Drs. Mary-Ellen Meadows and Dorene Rentz have been wonderful colleagues since the early days of our Brigham incarnation.

Drs. Kirk Daffner, Wes Farris, Margaret O'Connor, and David Wolk each read various chapters in preparation and provided astute commentary, helping me think through many complex issues. Margaret, in particular, has been my most candid reviewer and has probably forgotten more about memory than I will ever know.

David Diamond, Evan Kaplan, and David Rubinstein have all provided wise counsel and exceptional camaraderie; each is a best friend.

I am deeply grateful to Susan Gilbert, my collaborator on this project, whose patience and can-do approach helped me almost meet a few of my deadlines.

My work would be meaningless without my patients and their families, who continue to teach me about remarkable courage in the face of adversity and the affirmation of the human spirit. The enthusiasm of my postdoctoral fellows, graduate students, and clinical assistants (Dr. Meghan Searl, Dr. Aaron Hervey, Mimi Boer, Karen Sullivan, Dmitry Meyerson, and Alyson Negreira) reminds me of the importance and excitement of the work we all do.

Most of all I am thankful for my family—Margaret, Julia, and Ava—who make all of the effort and long days worthwhile, and to whom I dedicate this book. They continue to teach me that it takes more than a good memory to have good memories.

—Aaron Nelson

Introduction

You Can Protect and Improve Your Memory

You probably picked this book up because you are concerned that you don't remember things as well as you used to. You may find it annoying or may even be worried that this is the beginning of a more serious decline. As chief of neuropsychology at Brigham and Women's Hospital, a teaching hospital of Harvard Medical School, I can tell you you're not alone. I've seen thousands of patients who are worried about their memory. Some of them have neurological diseases, but many more—especially those in their forties and fifties—are in good health and are functioning effectively at work and in their personal lives. Still, something's wrong.

Research indicates that up to 40 percent of people in this age group are concerned about their memory. It's often relatively minor bouts of forgetfulness that bring people to my office for an evaluation. "Sometimes I walk into the kitchen and forget why," one woman told me. "If I stand there for a minute or two, I usually remember. But not always."

Other patients speak of forgetting where they parked the car at the mall and drawing a blank when they have to enter their PIN number in the cash machine. Some patients tell me that they have to reread passages in books over and over again because they just can't retain the information as well as they once could. Other patients confess to making errors at work—and fearing the consequences. "I was giving a presentation at our quarterly sales meeting and my vice president asked a basic question about our overseas activity," said a man in his fifties who works as an account manager for a major electronics company. "The answer should have been at my fingertips, but I couldn't come up with it; I just froze."

I'm not going to kid you. I worry about memory lapses just as you probably do. Here's something that happened to my wife (who heads a neuropsychology service at another Harvard-affiliated medical center) and me. We were about fifty miles from home, driving on a vacation trip, when our six-year-old daughter started looking for her "blankie," which we'd left behind. Rather than face a week of our daughter's rage and despair, we went back home to retrieve her prized possession. Thank goodness we did. When we pulled into our driveway, we were shocked to find that we'd left a set of keys in our other car—with the engine running!

As a memory doctor, I know that experiences like the ones I've just mentioned usually don't mean the beginnings of a degenerative brain disorder, such as Alzheimer's disease. More important, there are plenty of things you can do to strengthen your memory. This book will tell you why you have more trouble remembering things as you age and what you can do about it. It will describe simple things you can do to help prevent memory loss, whether due to aging or illness. The book will also reveal new findings about the brain and discuss new treatments for memory disorders.

Some Memory Loss Is a Normal Part of Aging

Just as your eyes don't see as clearly as they used to and your hearing isn't quite as sharp (could have something to do with all those 130-decibel rock concerts you flocked to in your younger days), your brain's memory operations decline somewhat as you age. Age-related memory loss isn't a disease but rather the result of normal changes in the structure and function of the brain that occur with age. These changes affect how well you concentrate, how quickly you process information, how effectively you store memories, and how easily you can recall them. These effects become particularly noticeable starting at around age fifty.

If this sounds like bad news, it's really not. For one thing, memory loss that's due strictly to the aging process is relatively minor. I don't mean to make light of the frustration and embarrassment that you and I feel when we forget something that we know we should remember. But age-related memory problems aren't so severe and frequent that they truly interfere with your ability to function normally in your daily life—that is, to do your job or manage your responsibilities at home. More important, you can guard against many of these problems with simple strategies to improve your ability to concentrate, commit information to memory, and recall it later on. These strategies have worked for my patients and for me, and they can work for you, too.

Optimal Memory Is a Function of Optimal Health

A few years ago, I had a consultation with a fifty-five-year-old executive who had noticed a pronounced decrease in his ability to multitask and retain details related to his work. Testing showed that he was having particular difficulty with attention and concentration—functions that are crucial for effective memory. He had no psychiatric disorder or neurological disease, but he did have a condition that most people don't think of as having anything to do with memory: obstructive sleep apnea.

Obstructive sleep apnea is a highly common condition in which breathing is disordered during sleep, leading to hundreds of "mini awakenings," which fragment the sleep cycle. People with obstructive sleep apnea can sleep for eight to ten hours or more and yet wake feeling unrested and unprepared to meet the day. Because people with sleep apnea are less alert, they are less able to process information and therefore to learn and remember. Once we brought my patient's obstructive sleep apnea under control, his ability to focus his attention and concentrate—and therefore to learn and remember information—improved.

As this vignette illustrates, Alzheimer's disease isn't the only cause of memory loss. Many more common—and treatable—conditions can cause forgetfulness, difficulty concentrating, and related problems. Many of these conditions become more common with age, such as hypertension, high cholesterol, thyroid disease, and, as already discussed, obstructive sleep apnea. Others can occur at almost any age, including depression, alcoholism, insomnia, and drug abuse. Still other contributors to memory problems are bad health habits, such as smoking, poor nutrition, and a sedentary lifestyle. Improving your health habits and getting proper treatment for medical and psychological conditions can help restore and optimize your cognitive function. What's good for your general health is good for your memory.

Brain Fitness

Scientists are now talking about "brain fitness" the way they've long talked about cardiovascular fitness. Let me explain. We've known for decades that there are many things that you can do to keep your heart and blood vessels healthy. Controlling blood pressure and cholesterol, not smoking, eating a diet that's low in saturated fats and trans fatty acids, and exercising regularly are proven ways to reduce your risk of heart disease and stroke. It turns out that essentially every single lifestyle factor that benefits cardiovascular health also benefits brain health. This is no surprise because the brain is highly dependent upon nutrition and energy derived from what we eat and that are delivered through the vascular system. Now researchers are identifying other ways to keep your brain agile and strong so that you can reduce or even reverse the types of memory lapses that are common with age.

While it's true that the quality of your memory is determined, in part, by your genes (choosing your parents wisely could really help!), preservation of optimal brain condition and function depends on numerous factors, many of which are within your direct control. Optimizing these factors amounts to establishing good habits early in life and sticking with them for the long term. Here are some of the most important things you can do:

- **Prevent or control hypertension and hyperlipidemia.**
  What's bad for the heart is definitely bad for the brain. By

damaging the tiniest blood vessels, hypertension and high cholesterol diminish the supply of nutrients that the brain depends on to function. What you can do is eat a well-balanced, heart-healthy diet. Dr. Walter Willett's book *Eat, Drink, and Be Healthy: The Harvard Medical School Guide to Healthy Eating* (2001) is an excellent reference in this regard.

- **Engage in regular cardiovascular, or aerobic, exercise thirty to forty-five minutes per day, at least four days per week.** There is an increasing body of evidence demonstrating the beneficial impact of aerobic activity on brain health and cortical plasticity, the capacity of the brain to sprout new neurons (brain cells) and form newer and denser interconnections among neurons, both of which help your memory.

- **Go easy on alcohol.** Research suggests a beneficial effect of moderate alcohol consumption (one or two beverages per day) on cardiovascular health. But when consumed in excess, alcohol can be toxic to neurons and lead to nutritional deficiencies.

- **Get a good night's sleep.** For most of us, that means approximately eight hours, although the need for sleep can vary among individuals and across the life span. Some interesting research in the past few years suggests that sufficient good quality sleep is instrumental in helping the brain consolidate new learning—a critical aspect of long-term memory. Good sleep means restorative sleep. If you have trouble with either the quantity or quality of your sleep, consult your doctor.

- **Manage stress.** Living with some degree of stress is a part of the human condition. At moderate levels, stress can actually enhance cognitive function by putting you on alert and preparing you to focus your full attention on a task. But too much stress overwhelms the brain's capacity to maintain attention and, over time, actually leads to the degradation of cognitive function. Prolonged stress is also associated with high levels of the hormone cortisol, which can damage regions within the brain that are critical for memory function.

- **Consider taking vitamins.** Judicious use of antioxidant supplements, such as vitamin C, has been associated with decreased levels of free radicals (substances produced in the body and brain that can have neurotoxic effects). Make sure you get enough of the B vitamins; deficiencies can contribute to memory loss.

- **Minimize your use of benzodiazepines and other prescription medications that have known adverse effects on brain function.** Talk with your doctor and work together to find alternative treatment strategies whenever possible.

- **Take care in using over-the-counter medicines, too.** Many of the most widely used over-the-counter medicines can also interfere with mental function because of their effect on brain neurotransmitters, as well as their interactions with prescription medications and even herbal supplements. They include antihistamines, antacids, and sleep medicines. Learn about the side effect profiles of these medications and discuss them with your doctor.

- **Keep learning new things**—new skills, new sports, new hobbies, new areas of personal research interest. The use-it-or-lose-it notion definitely applies to the brain.

- **Minimize passive activities, such as watching TV.** Although TV viewing can be construed as a form of mental activity, research suggests that people who watch relatively greater amounts of TV generally enjoy poorer physical and cognitive health.

- **Maintain a sense of psychological engagement in life.** This is one of the most important and least appreciated factors in optimizing brain health. Find out what it is that makes your life important—whether it's family, friends, the pursuit of a goal, or possibly even commitment to an idea or a faith. Although the substance of this engagement may evolve across the life span, the sense of maintaining a vital connection to something that matters can be constant.

New Treatments for Memory Problems

Our knowledge of the underlying process of establishing and recalling memories is evolving rapidly. We're making tremendous strides in understanding how the brain works. We're discovering genes that affect how memory changes with age, as well as your risk of developing memory disorders, such as Alzheimer's disease. We're also learning how stress hormones and reproductive hormones act on the brain and influence the processes of learning and remembering. These findings help explain why you probably have difficulties thinking when you're under stress. They also shed light on the memory problems that many women experience during and after menopause and that can plague men whose testosterone levels are low. This book will bring you up to date on the latest research on memory.

What we're learning about the brain is also leading to the development of treatments that enhance memory. As I write, there are five drugs approved by the Food and Drug Administration (FDA) for the treatment of Alzheimer's disease: donepezil (Aricept), galantamine (Reminyl), memantine (Namenda), rivastigmine (Exelon), and tacrine (Cognex). More of these medications are on the way. Research is investigating the use of these drugs in treating a less severe memory disorder called mild cognitive impairment. Now that it's possible to use medicine to enhance the pathways of memory in the brain, a new door has been opened: it may well be possible to use drugs to make a good memory even better. Indeed, an emerging trend is the use of these drugs (as well as herbal supplements) by healthy people in the hopes of boosting their memories beyond normal limits.

This might sound like a good idea, and maybe, ultimately, memory enhancers will be developed that are a boon to all of us. But there's a lot that we don't know, and I'm concerned about potential problems. Like steroids and other substances used by athletes to enhance physical performance, the proliferation of "cognitive enhancers" raises a host of legal and ethical issues, as well as safety concerns, which I discuss in this book. In some instances, an FDA-approved medication might be used for an unintended purpose; in other instances, an unapproved substance is put forward as a panacea. I hope you'll consider these issues if you're tempted by any of the drugs and supplements sold on the Internet that promise to endow you with "superhuman" memory.

The focus of this book is the same as my focus as a doctor—to help you make your memory as good as it can possibly be. The strategies and treatments discussed here work. They're not difficult to use, and they're not expensive. They make use of what we know about how the brain processes information and makes new memories. No matter how old you are, there are actions you can take to minimize age-related memory loss, prevent the potentially devastating impacts of common diseases, and reverse some of the damage that's been done. In other words, you can optimize your memory.

CHAPTER 1

What Is Memory?

When we talk about memory, we mean not only all that we remember but also our capacity for remembering. You might think that an optimal memory is a huge database that faithfully records and securely stores all that you have learned and experienced in your life. But actually, that wouldn't be optimal at all.

Not all memories are created equal. Some are meant to be retained for just a short time and then discarded. Imagine if you carried in your head every phone number you ever dialed or the time and location of every movie you ever saw. These memories would clutter your mind and, like outdated clothing in the closet or junk accumulated in the garage, they would make it harder for you to find the things that you need.

Memories that are important or emotionally powerful are stored in the brain for the long haul. This information is so ingrained that it is a part of you—images, experiences, and knowledge that have become intrinsic aspects of your psychological and social identity. Your memory includes facts and images, like the names of close friends and the faces of loved ones. It also includes procedures and skills, like how to drive a car or swing a golf club, and the specialized knowledge that you use for your work. It's when we start to forget these important things that most of us begin to worry.

The process of learning new information, storing it, and then retrieving it involves a complex interplay of brain functions. Understanding this process can help you appreciate why some memories endure and others fade away. Different parts of the brain play a role in whether you remember something over the short term or the long term.

Short-Term Memory

Short-term memory is information that you need to remember for just a few seconds or minutes. After that, it vanishes. It's the date and time of an appointment you just made—and must remember until you write it down in your calendar or personal digital assistant (PDA). *Working memory* is a form of short-term memory that's a bit more complex. Working memory comprises information that you hold in mind for a brief time to use for some specific purpose. Think of working memory in terms of your computer—as information that you need to keep up and running in an attentional window.

Working memory comes into play, for example, when you have to consider certain options and then make a decision fairly quickly. Let's say you're in the supermarket and you're trying to decide whether it's more economical to buy the large size or the medium size of laundry detergent. You remember the price of each and then do a mental calculation of the price per ounce to decide which item to buy. By the time you turn down the next aisle, you've probably forgotten the prices because you no longer need this information.

Short-term memories are supposed to be fleeting. They turn over at a high rate because new ones are continually replacing them, and there is only so much information you can keep in mind at once. Research shows that most people can hold only about five to nine unrelated bits of information in mind. That's why it's easier to remember a seven-digit phone number than a much longer number, such as the account number on your credit card.

Test Your Short-Term Memory

An excellent way to test your short-term memory is to see how many numbers you can remember either in a sequence or in reverse sequence. The more numbers you can remember in the proper order (or in the reverse order), the better your short-term memory is. It's harder to remember numbers in reverse sequence because this involves using your working memory—the "scratch pad" of your short-term memory. You must first remember the numbers in sequence and then transpose them. Remembering eight or more numbers in sequence and seven or more in reverse sequence would be impressive.

Although this memory test and others in this book are part of a battery of tests that are used in clinical evaluation, I want to make it clear that taking these tests will not enable you to make a valid diagnosis on your own. Making a diagnosis is a complex process that takes into account a broad spectrum of information about you. The purpose of the memory tests in this book is to give you some indication of how various aspects of memory are assessed. If you are worried about your memory, it's important that you talk with your doctor about your concerns.

Digit Span Forward
First, have someone read the first—and shortest—sequence of numbers at a rate of one digit per second. Then, recite them back in the proper order. Repeat this routine with the next line of numbers and the one after that and so on, until you fail two series in a row. (You can do this test alone by reading each line of numbers and then covering them up and writing them down in order.)

4–6–3–9

5–9–4–2–7

8–1–5–1–9–0

6–3–9–2–0–6–7

(continued)

Test Your Short-Term Memory, *continued*

5–0–1–7–4–9–6–3

8–1–8–6–0–4–7–2–6

Digit Span Backward

This test is harder than the first one because you have to use your working memory to remember the proper sequence of numbers long enough to figure out the reverse order. Have someone read the first line of numbers. Then recite them back in reverse order. For example, for the sequence 5–8–2–4, the right answer is 4–2–8–5. (As with the previous test, you can also do this one on your own by reading a line of numbers and then covering it up and writing down the numbers in reverse sequence.)

5–8–2–4

6–0–5–1–8

9–2–6–2–3–7

7–8–4–7–3–1–9

5–9–6–9–3–8–2–0

You can get a sense of how keen your short-term memory is by determining the longest numerical sequence you can remember. The longer the sequence, the better the memory. You can also use these tests to see how much your memory improves after you use the techniques I recommend in this book, especially the "chunking" strategy in Chapter 10.

The fleeting nature of short-term memory is actually beneficial because it allows you to discard unnecessary information. If you kept every short-term memory, your mind would become so overloaded with trivia that you would have trouble retrieving memories that are really important.

In his 1968 book, *The Mind of a Mnemonist: A Little Book About a Vast Memory*, the famous Russian neuropsychologist A. R. Luria describes a case in the scientific literature of a man (whom he calls S) who had a seemingly limitless capacity to remember detail—but this talent undermined his ability to lead a normal life. S retained so much information that he could not organize it into meaningful categories. He was utterly unable to set priorities, establish goals, and, really, live his life. In the end, S is a tragic figure, inhabiting a confusing world crammed with useless information and devoid of the meaningfulness and social connectedness that make life worth living.

Aside from having limited capacity, the brain system that handles short-term memory is also functionally fragile. Like a bubble that pops in a gentle breeze, a short-term memory is easily disturbed by interruptions. If you're trying to remember a phone number and someone walks into the room and asks you a question, chances are that you'll forget the phone number and have to look it up again. That additional information (the question) is sufficient to make the short-term memory vanish. To borrow another metaphor from computer technology, when new information enters the brain's short-term "buffer," older information is nudged out of the buffer and into cyberspace.

Long-Term Memory

Long-term memory consists of bits of information that your brain stores for more than a few minutes and then retrieves when needed. Put another way, long-term memory is the sum total of what you know: a compendium of data ranging from your name, address, and phone number and the names of friends and relatives to more complex information, such as the sounds and images of events that occurred decades ago. It includes the routine information that you use every day, like how to make coffee, operate your computer, and carry out all of the intricate behavioral sequences involved in performing your job or running your household.

The difference between short-term and long-term memory isn't just a matter of persistence but is also one of capacity—how much information the brain can handle. Although the brain can juggle only a few short-term memories at a time, its capacity for long-term memories is virtually limitless. Barring disease or injury, you can always learn and retain something new.

Long-term memories are also less fragile than short-term memories, which means that they remain more or less intact even when something interrupts your train of thought. I'll say more about the "more or less" aspect a little later on in the book. But as a preview, let me say that long-term memory is *not* like a video recording, such that a moment is captured and inscribed, forever unchanging, to be replayed identically the tenth time as well as the one thousandth. Memory for specific events and experiences is dynamic; it tends to change in both subtle and critical ways over time. As new experiences accrue and new memories are formed, older memories seem to shift and reconfigure, kaleidoscopically.

For example, you may have first encountered your future spouse decades earlier in an everyday interaction—a brief business meeting involving her company and yours. You were preoccupied with finalizing a major contract with a new client and barely noticed the woman sitting across the table. Three months later, you were introduced at a party and fell head over heels in love. You began dating and then married two years later. It's now your twentieth wedding anniversary, and you're reminiscing about how you met. You think back to the first encounter in the business setting—only when you think of it now, your memory is of being love-struck at that moment.

How you remember something is largely determined by who you are. Who you are reflects the interplay among a huge number of variables that form your personality. Add to that the totality of your lifetime of experiences and associated memories. To make matters even more complex, who you are changes to some extent across time. So what you remember and how you remember it will also change.

How you experience and then remember something is also shaped by your relative position in an unfolding event—your observational perspective. Your perspective is critical in determining what aspects of an event you attend to, as well as how you interpret them. Two people involved in an interaction are witnessing it from different perspectives. The specific observational perspective as well as the unique psychological makeup of each person will have a lot to do with how each participant perceives and remembers the interaction. This phenomenon has been dubbed the *Rashomon effect*, in acknowledgment of Akira Kurosawa's 1950 cinematic masterpiece *Rashomon*, which tells the story of an event from the perspective of four people who participated in it, each with a fundamentally different recollection of what happened.

Not all long-term memories last forever, even in a shifting state. Some long-term memories that go unused or become irrelevant fade over time. Have you ever read a book that you loved but years later found that you couldn't remember much more than the title? That's probably because you hadn't thought of the plot and characters in a long time. On the other hand, some long-term memories are amazingly persistent, no matter how infrequently you use them. Many adults I know are surprised by their ability to remember minute details of their childhood—an unjustified punishment they received, a fifth-grade science project, a room where they slept during a family vacation.

Your long-term memories fall into either of two general categories: *declarative memory* and *procedural memory*. Remembering the time and place of your lunch appointment next week (declarative memory) is different from remembering how to ride a bicycle (procedural memory). Declarative memory is more vulnerable to the effects of age, as well as of brain illnesses (such as Alzheimer's disease), than procedural memory.

Declarative Memory

Declarative memory includes information that requires you to make a conscious effort to recall. Another name for this type of long-term memory is explicit memory. There are two types of

Flashbulb Memory

Where were you at the moment you first heard about the attack on the World Trade Center? Whom did you talk with? What did you do next? All of the details that you recall constitute a flashbulb memory, a term that researchers use to describe an extremely vivid memory for an unexpected, emotionally charged public event. The assassination of President Kennedy, the *Challenger* space shuttle disaster, the September 11 terrorist attacks—images of these events became ingrained in the memories of millions of people who witnessed them, either directly or by means of television and other mass media.

Flashbulb memories tend to include numerous minute details of your experience of an event: weather conditions, what you were doing at the moment, who was near you, and so on. It's likely that the combination of profound meaningfulness and emotional impact surrounding the event helps sear it into your long-term memory. The psychological power of these types of events activates the amygdala, a structure within the brain's memory system that plays a major role in emotional processing.

It's long been assumed that flashbulb memories are more accurately and consistently maintained over time than are memories for ordinary experiences. But research shows that recollection of powerful events may also be vulnerable to distortion and reorganization over time.

A well-known study investigated long-term memory for the *Challenger* space shuttle explosion, which occurred in January 1986. One hundred six people completed a seven-item questionnaire one day after the tragedy regarding where they

declarative memory: *episodic* and *semantic*. Episodic memories are linked to events that occurred at specific times and in specific places. The party you attended last weekend, the vacation you took last summer, a movie you saw twenty years ago—these are all episodic memories, events bound in a specific temporal–spatial were, whom they were with, what they were doing, and so on, at the time they learned of the explosion. Approximately three years later, forty-four of the original participants were located and asked to respond to the exact same set of questions. The average accuracy score was three out of seven, and 25 percent of the respondents were wrong on every single item! Despite this low degree of accuracy, the participants rated their confidence in the correctness of their responses at greater than 4 on a 5-point scale.

More recently, scientists from Duke University compared people's memory for the events of 9/11 with their memory for other, ordinary episodes. The scientists asked people what they remembered about these two sets of events at intervals of one week, six weeks, and thirty-two weeks after they occurred. Although the study participants rated their 9/11 memories as much more vivid over time and believed that their recollections were more accurate than for the everyday episodic memories, the researchers found that the accuracy or consistency of the memories was similar for the two sets of events.

What this research tells us is that flashbulb memories are subject to the same biases and distortions that affect other long-term episodic memories. But even though they're imperfect, flashbulb memories are probably among the longest-lasting memories we have because they tend to be imbued with emotional significance and because they frequently entail catastrophic events that are kept in the public eye for an extended period of time. A flashbulb memory is re-evoked each time you see a reference to it in the newspaper, on TV, in a film, or in a history book.

context. When you revisit an event memory, you recall temporal information (when it happened) and spatial information (where it happened) about it.

Semantic memory is factual knowledge. Your semantic memory consists of much of the basic information you learned during your school days, along with an assortment of other facts, such as your mother's name, your address, or the meaning of the word *winter*. Unlike episodic memories, semantic memories aren't bound by time or place. You can't point to the moment when you learned your mother's name, for example. And even if you do know when you learned the multiplication tables or the name of the first president of the United States, the timing isn't important to your knowledge or recollection of these facts.

Procedural Memory

Procedural memory refers to, well, procedures: the skills and routines that you draw on automatically to perform actions like getting dressed, shuffling a deck of cards, or piloting a jet. Evidence of intact procedural memory is implied in the accurate performance of a skill or behavior. Even though your recall of procedural memories is relatively effortless, each one of them required effort and practice to learn. But ever since you mastered the skill involved, you've been able to perform it without necessarily remembering how you learned it or the separate steps entailed. When you take out your bicycle for a ride, you don't say to yourself, "OK, first I straddle the seat, then I put my left foot on the left pedal . . .," and so on. You just get on and go. It's as though your body does your thinking for you.

The old saying "You never forget how to ride a bike" appears to be largely true. Procedural memories don't fade or change much with age. You may feel a bit rusty if you haven't ridden a bicycle or played the piano in a while. But you don't have to relearn these skills all over again. With a bit of practice, the skills and routines come back to you. Even people with Alzheimer's disease can perform many routine tasks until the advanced stage of the illness. Scientists believe that procedural memory is robust because it is stored widely throughout the brain and because it is not dependent upon the hippocampus, one of the memory structures within the brain that is particularly vulnerable to the effects of normal aging.

Making Memories

Now that you know about the different types of memories and which ones are most likely to be affected by aging, we'll move on to the process of remembering. In Chapter 2, you'll learn step-by-step how memories are made in the brain: what happens when you first encounter new information, how the brain processes and stores that information, and how you are able to call up the information when you need it. You'll also learn some strategies for giving your memories staying power.

How You Remember

As you read this book, your brain is processing information, and if all goes well, you'll remember it for many years. But where, exactly, does this information go? One of the most enduring myths about memories is that they're stored in one place in the brain: a memory bank. Years ago, scientists assumed that you formed memories by depositing them in this bank and that you remembered things by withdrawing or borrowing them. Once you were finished using these memories, you returned them to the memory bank.

Although it was long suspected that this was not really the case, it was only about twenty years ago that scientists were able to prove that this assumption was wrong. Imaging technology became available that enabled us to get our first glimpse of the brain at work. The technology, called *functional brain imaging*, includes single photon emission computed tomography (SPECT), positron emission tomography (PET), and functional magnetic resonance imaging (fMRI). These methods allow researchers to see the brain at work by quantifying blood flow and tracking the brain's metabolism of certain substances in order to identify the regions that are most active during a particular type of mental activity. In other words, researchers can now see which part of the brain a person is using for different types of mental activity. This research has greatly increased our understanding of how memory works.

Your Brain's Memory Networks

When researchers used these imaging devices to study people's brains during their investigations of learning and memory, they observed that memories aren't stored in a single location, or memory bank, but rather are widely distributed in different networks of *neurons* (brain cells) throughout the brain. Most of these networks reside in the *cerebral cortex*, which is the outer layer of the brain's two hemispheres and the most highly developed part of the human nervous system. The cortex contains about twenty billion neurons that make possible all of the complex thinking and activity that you do. The anatomy of a neuron is shown in Figure 2.1.

Most of your neurons are highly specialized, responding selectively to only certain types of input. For example, some neurons become activated, or "fire," only in response to the movement of an object across your visual field in a particular direction. So these neurons would respond to a dog running from your neighbor's yard into yours but not going in the opposite direction. Other neurons respond only to sounds of a particular tonal pitch, while still others respond to salty tastes but not sweet tastes. Neurons in other brain regions control your voluntary movements—everything from walking to starting the car to playing piano. And other groups of neurons enable you to speak, write, and make decisions.

We've long known that different areas of the brain specialize in processing different kinds of information. For example, in more than 90 percent of people, language skills are concentrated in the left frontal and temporal lobes of the brain, and "seeing" (really, the brain's registration of visual images relayed from the eyes) occurs in the occipital lobes in the back of the brain. Other data, for example, derived from hearing, smell, and the analysis of spatial information (things like finding your way around town or playing chess), are processed in other regions.

What does all this have to do with memory? It suggests that a single memory is not stored in a single place, like a book on a shelf. Instead, your brain breaks down a memory into its informational components and routes each type of information to the

FIGURE 2.1 Anatomy of a Neuron

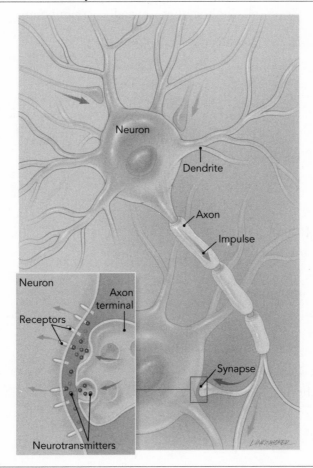

area of the brain that is specialized for processing it. Let's take an apple, for example. Your memory of an apple consists of how it looks, how it tastes, how it sounds when you bite into it, and so on. Each of these qualities of an apple is stored in a different place in your brain. Its visual form is stored in the occipital lobe. How it tastes is stored in the gustatory cortex in the insula and the amygdala. The sound of its crunch is stored in the temporal lobes. And its name is stored in the left temporal and parietal lobes. When you want to retrieve your memory of an apple, all of these brain regions become activated and work in concert to recombine

15

the "experience" of apple into a complete whole, like instruments in an orchestra playing together to produce a symphony.

That's not all. Each memory is connected to many related memories. For instance, if you associate apple with your mother's apple pies and Thanksgiving, each of these memories will be cross-referenced. With such a vast network for storing memories, your brain is like the Internet. Calling up memories is like doing an Internet search, with one or two words activating dozens or even hundreds of hyperlinks.

To get a sense of how far ranging these hyperlinks can be, try playing the game Six Degrees of Kevin Bacon. The basic objective is to connect another actor (or any well-known person) to Kevin Bacon through a series of no more than six links. This game turns out to be quite easy for movie buffs, who are able to connect the most obscure film producer from the 1930s to Kevin Bacon through a series of links.

Memory works a bit like this game. Your individual memories are situated within an amazingly dense network of associations and connections in which a tiny bit of experience can release a virtual cascade of recollection. We've all had the experience of remembering something that seems to come out of the blue, only to realize after reflecting that some seemingly trivial figment of a thought or an image triggered the memory.

Three Stages of Memory

But just how does the information that you see, hear, and learn on a daily basis get filed away? We're not entirely sure, but a few models have been proposed. The first one, devised in the 1960s, proposed that new learning proceeded in three distinct stages. First, the brain would register the sensory experiences (what you see, hear, smell, and so on), then the memory would go into a short-term storage system, and finally, the memory would either be transferred into a long-term memory store or discarded because it was not deemed important enough for long-term storage. Studies of people with amnesia have focused on stages of learning, and these stages proceed in a sequence of acquisition (registration), consolidation (storage), and retrieval. Current clinical tests of memory also use these three stages. A problem in any of them can interfere with memory function.

Stage 1: Acquisition

To remember anything, you first have to "acquire" it. When you are learning something, it is initially encoded in the form of temporary pathways of neuronal activation in your brain. *Neuronal activation* refers to a pattern of nerve cell "firing" in which nerve cells, or neurons, communicate with each other. The paths are forged by the communication of one neuron with the next.

The location of these pathways depends on the nature of the information being processed. For example, if you're studying a map to figure out how to get somewhere, the pathway will probably recruit neurons from the right parietal lobe, an area of the cortex that processes spatial information. If you're listening to someone speak, a pathway will form in the left temporal lobe, which processes language.

Keep in mind that the pathways that represent what you've just experienced are temporary, which means that the information is part of your short-term memory system. Most of this information will quickly fade away. This is why you can look up a phone number, remember it on your trip from the phone book to the phone, but then forget it as soon as you've placed the call. The information that makes its way into your long-term memory is the information that you encoded most completely in the first place and that is strengthened over time through a process known as consolidation, which I'll discuss shortly. One of the most important things that determines how completely you encode new information is how well you focused your attention when you were initially acquiring it. So when you have trouble remembering something, it's often because you weren't concentrating and didn't acquire it very well in the first place.

One reason that many people have more trouble remembering things as they age is that they have more trouble concentrating.

As we age, we are (for a variety of reasons) more easily distracted by background noises and other interruptions. Though some people are naturally better than others at tuning out distractions, as a rule, the ability to maintain focused attention declines with age.

Think back to when you were a teenager. Could you study for an exam effectively with the stereo on and people talking in the next room? Today, when you're reading a book and then someone turns on music, do you have trouble concentrating? If so, that's because the words in the book and the music drifting into the room are competing for your attention and making it difficult for you to focus on either of them very well. In clinical neuropsychology, this is what we refer to as a divided attention task, which is the basis for some of the most notoriously difficult cognitive tests. Your attentional focus is in some ways like the lens of a video camera; it can see only one field of view at a time. You can shuttle back and forth between two locations, but the result will be that you will capture only partial information from each of them.

Fortunately, there are highly effective strategies that you can use to improve your ability to concentrate and acquire information. I've taught them to my patients with great success. You'll learn what they are and how to use them in Chapter 10.

Stage 2: Consolidation

Closely concentrating when you read or listen to someone speak increases the probability that you'll remember the information over the long term, but it's not a guarantee. For the information to become secured in long-term memory, the initial neural pathway must be strengthened. The strengthening process is called consolidation.

The consolidation process occurs over a period of minutes, hours, days, or even longer, depending on the nature and complexity of the information. Chemical and structural changes strengthen the neuronal pathways that were initially created during acquisition, making them more durable. These chemical and structural changes also bolster the information so that it resists interference from other information and disruptive influences.

Ultimately, the consolidation of newly acquired memories leads to the creation of new *synapses*, the junctions between two neurons across which *neurotransmitters* (chemicals that regulate neuronal communication) carry messages. Increases in this chemical connectivity lead, in turn, to the sprouting of the billions of infinitesimally small branchlike neuronal projections, the *axons* and *dendrites*, which send and receive these chemical messages.

What determines if a short-term memory will be effectively consolidated into a longer-term memory? Several factors come into play, including how well you sleep, as you'll see in the following sections.

Consolidation of Declarative Memories. The consolidation of declarative memories—such as names and faces—is mediated by the *hippocampus*, a seahorse-shaped structure deep within the limbic system of the brain. The hippocampus becomes activated during the consolidation of important information. Consolidation entails the replay and rehearsal of the sequence of events to be remembered, thereby strengthening the pattern of neuronal activation. The hippocampus and other limbic system structures that play a role in memory consolidation are shown in Figure 2.2.

The hippocampus is selective with regard to the information that it consolidates. Several factors influence whether the hippocampus responds to new information and gives the signal to store it as a long-term memory. For one thing, you're more likely to retain new information if it relates to long-term memories that are already established. If you follow professional baseball, for example, you will have an easier time remembering details about recent team statistics and players than someone who's not interested in the sport. Another factor that influences consolidation is the emotional impact of the information. You're far more likely to remember a photograph or story that's disturbing (an image or a description of an anguished victim of war, for example) or joyful (two lovers embracing) than one that's bland (a newspaper ad for a vacuum cleaner). The part of the limbic system that reacts most directly to emotionally powerful information is the amyg-

19

FIGURE 2.2 Limbic System

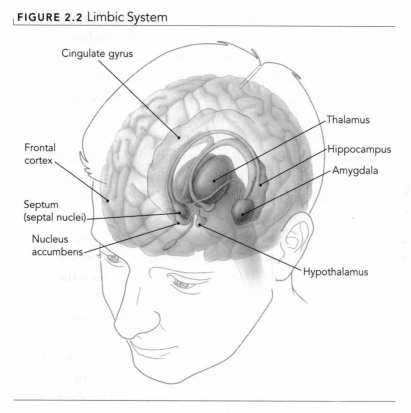

dala, situated right next to the hippocampus. Research using PET scans shows that information that activates the amygdala is more likely to be retained over the long term.

A good night's sleep appears to be important for memory consolidation. Several studies have shown that people remember word lists, spatial information, and visual and motor tasks better if they sleep after acquiring the information. Sleep might also help you recover new memories that faded during the previous day.

In a study published in the journal *Nature* in 2003, people learned new words and word sounds and were tested periodically throughout the day to see how well they retained the information. Predictably, they recalled most of the novel words and sounds soon after learning them, but as the day wore on, they recalled fewer and fewer of them. After awakening the following morning, however, the people's memories had rebounded—they recalled as many of the words and sounds as they had immediately after learning them the previous day. Clearly, something happened during sleep to render the memories more accessible and stable.

Why would sleep make such a big difference in how we remember? It seems that the connections between neurons, which support each memory, are strengthened when we sleep. In research with rodents, researchers at the Massachusetts Institute of Technology have shown that during the nondreaming stage of sleep, the pattern of neuronal firing in the hippocampus is similar to the activity that appeared earlier during the learning episode. This finding suggests that during nondreaming sleep, the hippocampus strengthens the pattern by playing it over and over again. The replay of the newly learned information is thought to be a key component of the consolidation process.

Dreaming may also play a role in memory consolidation. Research shows that during the stage of sleep when dreaming occurs—called rapid eye movement, or REM, sleep—there's increased activity in areas of the neocortex where most memories are thought to be stored. We all dream occasionally about events or experiences from the day before. Generating such dreams may well be a strategy that the brain uses to strengthen the neuronal pathways that make a memory remain with you. Dr. Robert Stickgold and his colleagues from Harvard Medical School, who study dreaming and memory, believe that when you dream, the hippocampus and the cortex are shuttling information back and forth—in essence, transferring information from the brain region (the hippocampus) that's first involved in learning to areas of the brain (the cortex) that will store the information over the long term.

Consolidation of Procedural Memories. Skills you acquire—like learning how to serve a tennis ball, playing a computer game, or coordinating the left and right hands to play the piano—are considered procedural memories and are consolidated differently from declarative memories.

21

Although research has revealed less about the consolidation of procedural memories than the consolidation of declarative memories, we do know that procedural memory doesn't depend on the hippocampus. People who have amnesia and have damage to the hippocampus have trouble forming new declarative memories but are capable of learning new skills, procedural memories, through practice. This phenomenon—improved behavioral performance even when a person can't remember learning the skill—has been dubbed learning without awareness.

We also know that procedural memory is distributed widely throughout the brain in regions including the frontal lobes, the cerebellum, and the basal ganglia. These structures are important for motor function (your ability to move) and communicate with your muscles to coordinate your body's movements. Because these brain structures are less vulnerable to the aging process and degenerative disorders such as Alzheimer's disease, procedural memory remains relatively intact across the life span. The hippocampus, on the other hand, does change with age and is devastated in the setting of Alzheimer's disease. It stands to reason, then, that the memories that become more difficult to recall when you get into your forties and fifties are the memories that are mediated by the hippocampus: people's names, appointments you've made, and other declarative memories. Procedural memories, on the other hand, are relatively robust. You are less likely to forget how to ride a bicycle or play the piano.

Recent studies strongly suggest that sleep also helps consolidate procedural memory and that a good night's sleep is essential for you to learn to perform any motor tasks well. Researchers have divided sleep into a number of stages, largely based upon their respective patterns of brain electrical activity. Sufficient amounts of specific stages of sleep appear to be critical for the consolidation of procedural memory.

Dr. Stickgold and his colleagues at Harvard conducted an experiment in which students played a computer game and then, over the following days, were tested on how well they remembered the game. Students who had more than six hours of sleep the night after they learned the game remembered it better the next day than did students who had less sleep. Again, specific phases of sleep were critical for effective learning. Even two days to a week later, students who were well rested outperformed those who hadn't slept as well.

Stage 3: Retrieval

Retrieval is the act of recalling something. As I mentioned earlier, each memory resides in a unique pattern of neuronal activation in your brain. To retrieve information, your brain must reactivate the pattern.

Similar memories have partially overlapping patterns of neuronal activation. Occasionally when you try to retrieve one memory, a similar memory comes to mind and blocks the information you want. You might try to remember the name of a song, but instead you remember the name of the singer who recorded the song or the name of a movie that featured it.

It takes less than a second to reactivate a neuronal pathway that holds simple or highly familiar information, like your phone number or the image of your father's face. In studies of face processing in which people are asked to decide whether photographed faces are familiar or unfamiliar, it takes about a fifth of a second for the image to reach the area of the brain that processes visual information and another fifth of a second for the person to decide whether the image is familiar.

If it always took just a fraction of a second to remember something, you wouldn't worry about your memory. But as we all know, it often takes much longer. Even if there's nothing wrong with your memory, it can take several seconds or more to recall complex information. See how long it takes you to determine the square root of 169. Depending on your proficiency with math, you might first need to activate the neuronal pathway that holds the definition of *square root* and then activate pathways that enable you to calculate the answer, 13. You can survey your recall of information from other domains, such as the number of U.S. presidents with the last name of Johnson, books written by Jane

23

Austen, or films that won the Academy Award for best picture over the last five years.

The more often you retrieve a piece of information, the easier it is for you to find it the next time. Information that you haven't retrieved lately might take a while to recall, or you may not be able to retrieve it without the help of a cue, a bit of information that triggers the recollection of other information. As you age, you accumulate more and more information that remains "unrecalled" for longer and longer periods of time. In the process of retrieving a fact such as a specific word or someone's name, you might struggle for seconds or minutes, feeling that the answer is on the tip of your tongue. If the neuronal pathways in your brain leading to the answer are still intact, chances are that you'll eventually retrieve it.

It's tempting to think of the process of retrieving memories as akin to taking a book off a shelf, but it's not. A book's content remains the same, but your memories don't. Memories change somewhat over time in response to new experiences. That's because your brain itself is also an ongoing work in progress. Each time you have a conversation or learn something or go somewhere, neural pathways in your brain are reconfigured. Some connections are strengthened and others weakened; these changes tweak and embellish and, in some cases, erode the memories that have been stored in your brain.

Researchers used to assume that once a memory was consolidated into the long-term memory system, it had become so durable that it couldn't be lost or altered by subsequent experience the way short-term memories are. However, new research suggests that when you recall consolidated memories, they temporarily become fragile again. In this fragile state, they are vulnerable to being altered or partially lost by interruptions and intrusions from other data that are swirling around your brain, such as sensory input, thoughts, feelings, and other memories.

Some memory scientists now believe that after you retrieve a memory, your brain has to consolidate it again. If this is true, it could be yet another factor that explains age-related memory loss.

As the hippocampus ages, it becomes less adept not only at consolidating new memories but also perhaps at reconsolidating old ones.

Test Your Visual Memory

This exercise assesses your immediate recall of visual information and how much visual detail you retain over a longer period. First, study the design in Figure 2.3 for fifteen seconds. Then cover the page and draw the design from memory. Don't look at the original design again just yet. After doing something else for thirty minutes, draw the design again. Now compare your two drawings to the

FIGURE 2.3 Visual Memory Test

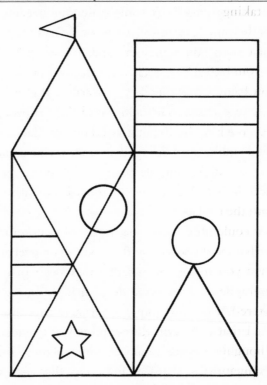

(continued)

Test Your Visual Memory, *continued*

original. How accurate was your first drawing? How accurate was the second?

Although neuropsychologists rely on standardized scoring and interpretive criteria to score this type of test, you can get a general assessment of your visual memory by seeing how much of the design you remember over time. Most people forget small details of the figure the second time around but remember the large features. The more detail you can remember, the better your visual memory is.

Memories That Last

Most of my patients don't come to see me because they've forgotten how to make a pot of coffee or ride a bicycle. These skills are forms of procedural memory and, as I mentioned earlier, procedural memory remains relatively intact as you age. Patients tend to come see me when they begin to forget things like important dates, tasks they have to do, and even names of people they know well. It's these kinds of declarative memories that can become elusive when you're middle-aged or older. But some declarative memories are more durable than others. Remember, there are two subtypes of declarative memory: semantic (factual) and episodic (event-related).

Specifically, information that is part of your semantic memory (the strictly factual knowledge that you call up over and over again, such as your spouse's name, what 5 times 4 equals, and the knowledge base that you draw on to do your job) is more resilient than episodic memories (the unique event memories that are linked to a point in time, such as the dinner party you attended last month). Even though both episodic and semantic memory initially depend on the hippocampus, there are important differences. Because we tend to access and use semantic memories more often, they tend to be more durable. Certainly, many semantic memories do fade, like

Recipe for a Lasting Memory

Ingredients

- Begin with a unique experience—something that stands out from mundane everyday life.
- Have the experience engage all of the senses:

    Vision

    Hearing

    Taste

    Smell

    Touch

- Make it meaningful—something that you connect with and that engages your interest.
- Add a dash of emotional salience—not too much and not too little. (Too much emotion can interfere with your memory, whereas too little emotion can make information so dull that it is unmemorable.)

Steps

1. Focus your attention fully and single-mindedly.
2. Actively process the experience as it is occurring; create an association between the new experience and an established memory.
3. Rehearse and replay the experience at different times and in different places. Talk about it with others and think about it on your own immediately afterward and from time to time thereafter.
4. Get a good night's sleep.

    Enjoy for a lifetime!

the plots of novels and movies that you've seen, but these tend to be the memories that you don't use very much.

Episodic memories are more fragile because you're not as likely to recall them as often as information that you use every day. An episodic memory is far more specific than semantic information, being a one-of-a-kind event that occurred in a singular place and time. For example, you can probably remember that a city named Burlington is located in Vermont (a semantic memory). This is general knowledge; you don't need to remember who first told you about Burlington, Vermont, or where you were when you first learned of it. You just know it. But you're more apt to struggle to remember a lunch you had at a McDonald's on June 8, 1995, in Burlington (an episodic memory). Why? Because this type of event overlaps with other similar events in the category of "lunches at McDonald's." Chances are you weren't straining to absorb all of the details around you at that McDonald's. And how often would you have recalled this specific episode over the years?

Certain subtypes of semantic memory appear to be particularly durable. There's some truth to the adage that you never forget a face. Some research shows that older people recall faces nearly as well as younger people do, although other studies suggest a significant decline in the ability of older people to remember other types of visual information, such as images or scenes.

Perhaps one reason that we tend to remember faces more easily than other visual information is that faces are linked to our emotions. You pay more attention to information that resonates with you emotionally than to information that leaves you cold. You also call emotionally linked information into conscious thought more often, and therefore, the neural network that supports it is more elaborate. It's no coincidence that the structures that govern memory and the structures that govern emotion are close together in the limbic system of the brain and share millions of reciprocal connections for facilitating two-way communication.

Your capacity for acquiring, consolidating, and retrieving memories is a wondrously complex and dynamic process. Next, you'll see what sorts of problems can gum up the works to distort some memories and erase part or all of others. The following chapters describe the differences between normal and abnormal memory loss, and tell you what you can do about them.

CHAPTER 3

It Happens to Everyone: Normal Memory Lapses and Distortions

It's normal to forget some things, and it's normal to become somewhat more forgetful as you age. "I couldn't find my purse when I came home from the supermarket the other day, so I drove back to the store in a panic. I was convinced it had been stolen!" a patient told me. "But when I got home and was unpacking the groceries, there it was in one of the shopping bags." This is a classic instance of absentmindedness, a memory lapse that's so much a part of the human condition it's the stuff of comedy skits.

Do you find that not only do you forget things but your mind also "plays tricks" on you? You feel so confident about your recollection of a particular event, only to discover that you are entirely wrong on one or more key details. Let's say you remember that your neighbor's daughter became engaged and you are sure that your neighbor told you this information. But it turns out that you'd actually read about it in the local newspaper. This is an example of misattribution, a memory error that happens to practically everyone and becomes more common with age.

Absentmindedness and misattribution are but two kinds of memory problems that are so common they're considered within the range of normal experience. Having occasional memory lapses is not a sign that you have a memory disorder. It's only when they occur regularly or when they come to involve more significant or familiar information that they're a cause for concern.

Schacter's Seven Sins

In his book *The Seven Sins of Memory* (2001), Daniel Schacter, a professor of psychology at Harvard University, reviews the most common types of problems that interfere with everyday memory function. These "sins" affect everyone some of the time; they don't just befall people with serious memory impairments.

Transience

You read the newspaper this morning, but you can't remember what the lead articles were. You attended a seminar six weeks ago, and even though you were fully engaged in the subject matter and found the lectures fascinating, you are now unable to recall the names of any of the presenters, let alone the points covered in the talks. You're doing a crossword puzzle and the cue for an answer is "Norman Mailer's first novel." Although you were a literature major and wrote your senior thesis on Mailer thirty years ago, you cannot come up with this basic fact about Norman Mailer.

These are all examples of transience, the tendency for memories to weaken over time. Memories that you call upon frequently can remain fairly vivid for decades, whereas others fade to the point of being lost altogether.

The period of time when you're most likely to forget information is soon after acquiring it. Information contained within the short-term memory system is, by definition, transient. Once information passes out of short-term memory and is consolidated into long-term memory, it assumes a more stable form, at least temporarily. Memory has a use-it-or-lose-it quality: you remember the things you think about most often. That's why the details of a book you read two years ago will remain more vivid if you periodically discuss the book with someone than if you simply leave it on your bookshelf.

Absentmindedness

Maybe you've never forgotten something as significant as turning off the ignition before getting out of your car, but certainly you've forgotten where you put your keys. That's a common example of absentmindedness, difficulty remembering a bit of information or an event because it didn't sufficiently register in the first place. Absentmindedness frequently results when you are trying to do two things at once and don't pay enough attention to either task. It can also occur when something or someone distracts you, pulling your focus away or fragmenting your concentration. You can't find your car keys (or your eyeglasses or your pen, and so on) because you didn't focus on where you put them when you came in the front door. Because you were thinking of something else (or, perhaps, nothing in particular), you didn't encode the information securely.

Forgetting an appointment or skipping a dose of medication—anything that involves doing something at a specific time—are other examples of absentmindedness. In these cases, it's likely that you didn't focus on cues that could remind you to follow through with a planned activity. If your doctor instructed you to take your medicine at bedtime and you forgot to do so, it could be that you didn't pay close enough attention to the key word: bedtime. If you had, chances are that certain details of your bedtime routine, such as brushing your teeth or watching a particular TV show, would have served as cues to remind you to take your medicine.

A Chinese proverb tells us that the palest ink is better than the best memory. Where appointments and schedules are concerned, the best cues are written reminders. It's unrealistic to expect that you will be able to keep your entire calendar in your head. It's not that the information is unimportant, but most relevant details, like dates and times, are simply too fleeting—and too "low contrast"—to store in long-term memory. And yet you probably won't use the information soon enough for short-term memory to be of any help.

When I see patients who complain about absentmindedness, I counsel them to keep all of their appointments and to-do lists on a calendar or in a PDA—and to cultivate a routine of reviewing this information at least three times each day (first thing in the morning, at midday, and in the evening). Anchoring the schedule check to usual mealtimes is an example of using a cue to increase the likelihood of remembering to enact a behavior. Once a person develops the habit of doing this, the problem usually resolves.

Blocking

Someone asks you a question and the answer is right on the tip of your tongue—you *know* that you know it, but you just can't think of it. This tip-of-the-tongue experience is probably the most familiar example of blocking, being unable to recall a specific memory because another memory is standing in the way. When you have this experience, your recall failure is not due to inattention or loss of the information from memory storage. On the contrary, blocking occurs when a memory is properly stored in your brain, but something is obscuring it, keeping you from finding it.

Often the memory block is another bit of information that overlaps the same "semantic space" as the information you're searching for. In other words, it possesses one or more of the key attributes of the sought-after information. This interfering memory is so intrusive that it gets in the way when you try to retrieve the memory you want. The harder you try to peer around the edge of this interloper, the more insistent it becomes at forcing its way into your consciousness. Let's say you're trying to think of James Dean's last movie (*Giant*), but *Rebel Without a Cause* keeps coming to mind. You know that this is the wrong answer. You also know that the right answer is *Giant*, but you can't think of it because *Rebel* is blocking the way.

A common example of blocking is when you call one of your children by the name of another. Convinced that this error is the first slip down a slippery slope that will end with failure to recognize their most beloved family members, more than one patient has broken into tears in my office. Many patients who come with this concern associate this type of innocuous error with the experience of a parent or grandparent with late-stage Alzheimer's disease, who eventually failed to recognize them. But occasionally calling one family member by another's name is not, in and of itself, a sign of a memory disorder.

Memory researchers refer to blocking memories as "ugly stepsisters" because they're domineering, like the stepsisters in *Cinderella*. Ugly stepsisters have been used in studies of memory. In one such experiment, people were given lists of uncommon words and asked to match them with lists of possible definitions. When choices included incorrect definitions that were similar to the accurate definitions, more people had memory blocks than when unrelated definitions were given.

Functional imaging studies provide a clue about how blocking might work. When you're retrieving a memory, some brain regions become more active and others become less active. Memory researchers interpret this finding to mean that the active regions inhibit the other regions. This inhibition can be advantageous, facilitating retrieval by preventing your brain from calling up the wrong information. But when you call up an ugly stepsister, the activated regions that held this blocking information might suppress the regions needed to retrieve the sought-after response.

Memory researchers believe that memory blocks become more common with age and may explain why older people often have difficulty remembering names. In any case, there's some encouraging news about blocking. Research shows that approximately half of the time people are able to retrieve a blocked memory within one minute.

Misattribution

Misattribution refers to mistaking the source of a specific memory. Misattribution can take many forms. You might have heard that a store in your neighborhood was closing and you may believe that you saw a sign about this in the store window. In reality there was no such sign; rather, a neighbor told you the news. Another type of misattribution occurs when you're convinced that a thought you had was totally original when, in fact, it came from something you'd read or heard. This sort of misattribution explains cases of unintended plagiarism, in which you write something that contains phrases or thoughts from an article or a book that you read. Misattribution can have profound consequences when witnesses to crimes—or members of the media—don't get their sources straight.

Like blocking, misattribution also seems to become more common with age. One reason is that the older you are, the older your memories are, and old memories, which have not been retrieved frequently and recently enough, are particularly prone to misattribution. As you age, you're also more likely to incorrectly attribute newly acquired memories because you are less able to encode and retain specific situational details and tend to rely more heavily on gist or general familiarity when forming a new memory. But make no mistake: misattribution happens to people of all ages. It can be frustrating and embarrassing, but it's usually not a sign of a memory disorder.

Two strategies can help cut down on misattribution. One strategy is to make a point of concentrating on details and specifics when you want to remember something important. As you focus on new information, ask yourself the five Ws: *Who* told me this? *What* was the content of the information? *Where* was I when I encountered this information? *When* did this happen? *Why* is this important to remember? This type of effortful, detail-oriented processing will reduce many types of inaccuracies, including misattribution.

Another strategy is to take a moment to mentally examine a memory when you first call it up before jumping to a conclusion about its source. Here's why. Misattribution often occurs when a piece of information is so familiar that you reflexively associate it with similar information that you already know without stopping to think whether the association is valid. Think back to the example I gave earlier about the store going out of business. It's understandable that you might assume you saw a going-out-of-business sign in the window because such signs are common at stores that are closing. But if you'd stopped to think about where you learned about this *particular* store closing, you'd have improved your odds of matching the information to its true source.

Suggestibility

Imagine that you're watching your child's soccer game and the other team scores a goal. A parent complains that the goal shouldn't count because the player who scored it touched the ball with her hands in violation of the rules. At the moment the goal was scored, you hadn't noticed that the player used her hands, but when your mind runs an instant replay of the action, you now *see* that she did.

Is your memory accurate? Did you actually see the foul? Did the foul even happen? The answer to all three questions is, not necessarily. Your memory for the play may have been influenced by suggestion. Suggestibility refers to the vulnerability of your memory to being influenced by information that you learn after the fact. The "latecomer" information insinuates itself into your memory the next time you recall the event.

Numerous studies have demonstrated how easy it is to implant "false memories" into people's recollection of their childhood. In one study, parents filled out a questionnaire that asked whether certain events happened to their children, who were now college students. The students themselves were then asked if they remembered certain events. Some of these events had actually occurred, according to the parents' questionnaires, but others were fabricated. At the time of the first rating, the majority of the students accurately distinguished between the true and false events. However, in later interviews, if a researcher suggested that a fabricated event had actually happened to them when they were children, 20 to 40 percent of the students described some memory of it.

We don't know if you become more vulnerable to suggestibility as you age, but we do know that it happens to people of all ages. Several studies with preschoolers indicate that suggestive questioning by the police or other authority figures can lead children to assert that certain events occurred when in fact they didn't. Notable memory researchers have questioned the accuracy of children's testimony in high-profile cases of alleged sexual abuse, such as the Fells Acres case in Massachusetts and the McMartin Preschool case in California, both of which gripped the nation in the 1980s. The children's "memories" were thought to have been influenced by leading questions and information to which the children were exposed during the investigative process.

Similarly, the credibility of "recovered memories" of childhood abuse has been called into question. In a typical case of recovered memory, an adult in psychotherapy may begin to experience memories of traumatic events related to very early childhood. Retrospective analysis of how some of these memories were unearthed has raised questions about possible suggestive techniques used in the therapy process.

Recovered Memories. Perhaps no other concept in contemporary memory science is more controversial than recovered memory. *Recovered memory* refers to the recall of a previously repressed memory. Repression is a psychological defense mechanism that forces a highly disturbing event out of conscious awareness in order to protect a person from anxiety. When a repressed memory emerges into consciousness, it is said to be a recovered memory.

Recovered memories are most often cited in cases of early childhood trauma in which the victim was assumed to have unconsciously repressed a horrific experience, keeping it locked away from conscious awareness for years. Proponents of recovered memory believe that the experience of the traumatic memory is provoked, either gradually or abruptly, by an event or another stimulus that the person consciously or unconsciously associates with the trauma. Sigmund Freud believed that repressed memory formed the basis for neurosis. Some psychotherapists facilitate the recovery of buried memories of traumatic events as a step toward emotional healing for their patients.

The debate over the validity of recovered memory is most intense in legal cases involving alleged abuse or horrendous crimes. In what has been cited as the first case in the United States of a murder conviction based on a recovered memory, George Franklin Sr., of Redwood City, California, was found guilty in 1990 of the rape and murder of an eight-year-old girl that had occurred twenty-one years earlier. The 1969 case was reopened after Franklin's daughter, Eileen, came forward, claiming to have recovered a vivid memory of witnessing her father committing the crime. By her report, Eileen's "memory" was triggered by an innocuous remark made by her young daughter. The case was later dismissed when it was learned that Eileen's recovered memories were based on facts that had been published in newspaper accounts at the time of the crime; hence, Eileen's "memory" of the event may have been based on misattribution.

Critics of the recovered memory concept argue that the same type of influences that create false memories can be at work in psychotherapy and in criminal investigations. The therapist's role as an authoritative figure provides powerful leverage for influencing the thoughts, feelings, and memories of the patient. A therapist can intentionally or unintentionally use the power of suggestion to induce a patient to think that he or she remembers something that didn't happen. And in criminal investigations, police, social workers, and other officials in positions of authority can dramatically influence what a person remembers.

Proponents of the recovered memory concept argue that the more unusual and disturbing the memory, the less likely it is to be false. They also contend that it is natural for many recovered memories to be revealed in therapy sessions because the therapist creates a safe environment in which disclosure is key to the efficacy of treatment.

At this point, there's no consensus regarding the validity of recovered memories. But as research clarifies how memory works, we'll gain a better understanding of the interplay between knowledge and emotion in the recollection of traumatic experiences and know with more certainty how useful and reliable recovered memories really are.

Bias

When you reflect on certain events in your life from several decades ago, what's your overall impression of them? Which details do you recall?

Try an experiment. Ask a friend from college to reminisce about your college graduation. Chances are that the two of you won't remember it in the same way. Let's say, for example, that you both remember the commencement speaker's name and that she was a journalist. But you remember the speech being dull and your friend remembers it being fascinating. You recall seeing your fellow graduates yawning and shuffling around from the tedium, but your friend remembers them being totally engaged.

Whose memory is more accurate? It's impossible to say because everyone's memory is subject to bias. Bias is the distortion of memory by the unique perspective of the rememberer. Your personality, your mood, your beliefs, and your experiences—everything that makes up who you are—will play a role in how you perceive and remember something. If your friend became a journalist and you became, say, a real estate developer, these differences might explain the differences in your memories of the commencement address. Bias colors your memories when they're first encoded and again when you retrieve them.

Bias will influence all sorts of memories, but among the most interesting examples are people's recollections of their romantic relationships. In one study, couples who were dating were asked to evaluate themselves, their partners, and their relationships. During a second session two months later, the couples were asked to recall what they'd said initially. The people whose feelings for their partners and their relationship had become more negative during the interval between the two study sessions recalled their initial evaluations as having been more negative than they really were. On the other hand, people whose feelings for their partners

Eyewitness Accounts: True or False?

Historically, eyewitness testimony has been considered one of the most powerful forms of evidence in criminal cases. After all, eyewitness testimony is, by definition, a firsthand account of an event by someone who was at the scene. But it turns out that eyewitness accounts are frequently inaccurate. An untold number of people in the United States have been convicted of crimes they did not commit—or acquitted of crimes that they did commit—because of memory errors.

The chief basis for inaccurate eyewitness accounts is suggestibility—an eyewitness to a crime acquires new information, or misinformation after the fact, by talking to other witnesses or reading descriptions in the press and then unknowingly incorporates this information into his or her own memory. The memory of an eyewitness is also subject to change under questioning by the police or lawyers. Dr. Elizabeth Loftus, a psychologist who has spent decades working with the criminal justice system on this issue, performed an experiment in which she showed people films of traffic accidents and then asked them to estimate how fast the cars were going. People gave higher estimated speeds when asked, "How fast were the cars going when they *smashed* into each other?" than when the question was phrased, "How fast were the cars going when they *hit* each other?" Dr. Loftus's memory research is being used to help police officers, lawyers, and judges become more aware of the processes involved and the problems with eyewitness testimony so that more valid investigative techniques can be developed.

and their relationships had become more loving recalled their initial evaluations as more positive than they really were.

We don't know if memory becomes more biased with age. But experiments like the one just described underscore the fact that memory doesn't work like a video recording, objectively memorializing your experience in an immutable form. So don't be concerned if someone tells you that you see the world through rose-colored glasses. Even the sharpest memory is not a flawless snapshot of reality.

Persistence

Most people worry about forgetting things, but sometimes you remember things that you wish you could forget. Persistence is the tendency to continually revisit a memory; it can be something mildly annoying like a song that sticks in your head or it can be a troubling or a traumatic event. Persistence often has an intrusive quality in the sense that you experience the disturbing recollection as a thought or an image that is forced into your awareness.

In the brain, persistent negative memories are thought to be mediated by the amygdala and other limbic areas that respond to fear, anxiety, and emotionally charged information. Several types of psychiatric disorders involve persistent, negative memories. Depression and persistent negative thoughts are linked in a vicious cycle; as the depressed person ruminates over real or imagined unpleasant events, his or her self-esteem erodes and the dysphoric mood deepens.

A symptom of many types of anxiety disorders is the persistent recall of a frightening event. Phobias, for example, frequently stem from an earlier encounter with an object or a situation that caused an overwhelming sense of fear. The visceral "memory" of the fearful encounter remains a persistent force, shaping the phobic person's behavior for years or decades.

A core feature of post-traumatic stress disorder (PTSD), a condition that can develop after a person experiences a traumatic event (for example, sexual assault or war), is the persistent intrusion of unwanted memories. With PTSD, persistent memories assume the form of flashbacks and nightmares of the traumatic event, causing a person to relive the ordeal. A flashback is a special form of memory in which the individual loses contact with present reality and is thrust back in time to the traumatic situation; the psychological distance that characterizes normal memory is lost.

Many people with phobias and PTSD learn to control persistent memories through therapy that involves guided imagery, or visualization. With this technique, a therapist helps the person learn to envision the object of the phobia or the traumatic incident in a graduated approach, which precludes the experience of intense fear. Once the emotional response to the stimulus diminishes, the memory of it becomes less persistent.

As for people without psychiatric disorders, what's the best way to eliminate a persistent memory? Don't try to ignore it. Research shows that willing yourself to avoid thinking about something makes you think of it all the more. It's better to let a persistent memory run its course. Eventually, it will intrude upon your consciousness less and less until it finally recedes altogether.

The Rashomon Effect

A concern voiced frequently by my patients has to do with their recall of a particular event that diverges widely from the recollection of someone else who was there. For example, a man I'll call Paul recently came to me for a consultation because he was extremely upset that he had been unable to remember an episode that occurred during a family Thanksgiving gathering two years ago. He and his sister were reminiscing and she mentioned the incident, characterizing it as a "knock-down, drag-out family fight." Paul had no memory of it happening. I encouraged him to check with other family members who were at the dinner to see if they recalled the event. When he next saw me, he announced with amazement—and relief—that virtually every person he spoke with provided a somewhat different account of what actually happened, including a brother who vaguely recalled a "lively discussion."

This form of bias is what I call the *Rashomon effect. Rashomon* is a classic film that tells the story of a violent crime from the viewpoints of four characters—among them, the alleged perpetrator and victim. Each account is different, reflecting each character's perspective during the event. What this movie renders so powerfully is the reality that memory is not an objective record of an event. What you perceive and remember is profoundly influenced by your unique observational perspective: where you were in relation to the event, how you were feeling at the time, what motivations and expectations you have, and who you are (the various quirks and characteristics that make up your personality). All of these factors combine to comprise a form of observational perspective bias.

An example of observational perspective bias would be that you and a colleague, when sitting on different sides of a table at a meeting, will be looking at different people and things and will come away from the meeting with different memories. You might see an account manager look bored or annoyed, but your colleague might miss this information if the manager's face is out of view. Or even if the manager's face is not hidden, your colleague might focus on different situational aspects, for example, the articulate, well-researched presentation given by another person. It stands to reason that you'd each remember different details from the meeting.

In addition to where you are physically situated, your perspective also depends on your social position. The boss will have a different point of view than a junior employee. A popular guest will have a different take on a party than someone who is not well known or well liked and has trouble finding someone to talk with. So don't worry if your recollection of an event is different from the recollection of someone else who was present. It's normal. Like your fingerprints, your memory is unique, because your experiences and perceptions are unique.

There are other memory problems that become more common with age because of changes in the structure and function of the brain. I discuss them in the next chapter.

CHAPTER 4

How Your Brain Ages

"I can no longer read," one fifty-five-year-old woman told me. "By the time I get to the end of a page, I've completely forgotten what I read a moment before. I end up rereading the same passage two or three times."

"Last week I rented a video," said a fifty-one-year-old man. "As I watched the movie, it seemed vaguely familiar. Finally, it began to dawn on me that I'd seen the movie before. It turns out I'd rented it just two weeks earlier!"

Can you tell which of these people has a brain disorder? The answer is, neither one. Both were reporting difficulties with attention, learning, and recall that are typical for people in middle age and older. Starting around age fifty, most people experience the following brain changes that directly affect memory and other cognitive functions:

- There is a decrease in the number of synapses, or "meeting points" between neurons.
- The number and functionality of *receptors* (the docking points on neurons where chemical messages are received) are diminished.
- Certain neurotransmitters (the chemical substances that regulate cell-to-cell communication) become less available to the brain for a variety of reasons.

- *White matter pathways* (the bundles of neuronal fibers that transmit messages throughout the central nervous system) develop lesions, or abnormalities, that can impair their functioning.

All of these changes slow down or interrupt the communication between neurons. I'll tell you more about these communication problems a little later in this chapter.

What Is Normal Aging?

Even in the face of these changes in brain structure and function, studies of successful aging in the oldest of the old, centenarians, have taught us that disruptive cognitive decline is not an inevitable part of the aging process. There is a tremendous range of variability in how we age. In fact, many neuroscientists disagree about the entire notion of normal aging.

At one end of the spectrum, there are researchers who view normal aging and degenerative brain diseases, such as Alzheimer's, as parts of a continuum. This view is supported by the finding that some people who do not exhibit memory problems during the aging process still have the hallmark biological features of Alzheimer's disease in their brains on autopsy. Although the extent of these disease features is substantially smaller than in people who exhibit memory problems, the presence of these features is viewed as evidence that each and every one of us would eventually develop Alzheimer's disease if we lived long enough.

At the other end of the spectrum are researchers who argue that the distinction between normal aging and disease is not simply a matter of degree. They maintain that disease is disease and normalcy is normalcy and ne'er the twain shall meet. This point of view is supported by the finding that there are many elderly people who continue into their nineties and beyond with only a subtle decline in memory. Furthermore, autopsy findings in some of these high-functioning elders reveal their brains to be surprisingly free of disease.

For our purposes, it doesn't really matter which side of the debate is right. Either way, you can still achieve an optimal memory. In the optimal approach, we focus on the best ways to preserve and enhance memory throughout life.

The Cycle of Neuronal Death and Neurogenesis

You may have heard the "fact" that you lose thousands of brain cells a day. For years, the scientific view of the adult brain was anything but encouraging. It was an unquestioned truth that your brain produced new brain cells only early in life and that upon reaching adulthood, your fixed complement of neurons would begin to dwindle. With this relentless cell death would come a sharp slide in your capacity to learn and think.

We now know that this position was a combination of exaggeration and half-truth. Though it's true that most of your brain's neuronal growth occurs during childhood and adolescence, you continue to grow new neurons throughout your life—a process known as *neurogenesis*. This capacity to produce new cells is a hallmark of the brain's *plasticity*, which allows it to continuously alter neural circuits and form new synaptic networks.

Granted, the rate of growth slows down considerably in adulthood, and you don't replace all that you lose. However, recent research suggests that in normal aging, there is no significant neuron loss in key areas of the hippocampus, the most important brain structure for memory. And we now know that the loss of neurons is at least partially offset by the sprouting of new brain cells, even within structures of the brain that are critical for memory. In fact, some researchers have concluded that neuronal density actually increases with age in some brain regions. Even if we assume a net loss of ten thousand neurons every day, it would take almost 274 years to lose 1 percent of your total neuronal complement.

Memory Myth: Once Brain Cells Die, They're Gone for Good

For years, scientists assumed that once you reached adulthood, you stopped growing new brain cells. In other words, they assumed that once brain cells died, they weren't replaced. But a few years ago, scientists found that adults do grow new brain cells. What's especially encouraging about this finding is that much of the new growth occurs in the hippocampus, the brain structure that's crucial for memory consolidation.

This finding has transformed the way neuroscientists think about the aging brain and memory. We now believe that, in most cases, no matter how old you are, your brain is capable of producing new brain cells that have the potential to support pathways that enable you to form new memories. And if the brain is able to generate new neurons, there's hope that one day it may be possible to offset the damage and severe memory loss brought on by degenerative brain disorders, such as Alzheimer's disease.

Communication Problems

Although we used to believe that age-related decline in memory was caused by a cumulative loss of neurons, more recent research has taught us that this is not the case. Experts now believe that the changes in the brain that play the most prominent role in age-related memory decline all bear on the brain's networking capability—the transmission of information from point to point via neurotransmitters, receptors, and synapses.

A structural change found in nonhuman primates is a reduction in the number of *dendritic spines* in a type of neuron called pyramidal cells. Spines are the filament-like branches that extend from neurons and create synapses with other neurons. It is almost certain that a reduction in spines also occurs in most aging humans as well. A loss of spines would directly cause a decrease in synaptic density, which, in turn, would diminish the degree of connectedness among neurons and thereby downsize the brain's information processing speed and capacity.

The loss of neurons in particular brain areas may hinder communication between cells by degrading the specific functions of those areas. The aging brain is vulnerable to loss of neurons in structures that produce neurotransmitters important for memory, including acetylcholine, dopamine, and serotonin. Fewer neurons in these areas can mean lower levels of these key neurotransmitters, leading to the type of problems that are familiar starting in middle age, such as trouble concentrating on and remembering what you're reading.

Let's take a closer look at other changes the brain undergoes beginning in middle age that interfere with the normal flow of information from neuron to neuron, making it harder for you to process information effectively, learn, and remember.

One is a change in the number and function of receptors, the docking points on neurons where neurotransmitters attach themselves when neurons send messages to each other. In several parts of the brain, there is a decrease in receptors for dopamine. Perhaps of greater importance is a decline in the function of receptors for NMDA (N-methyl-D-aspartate), which play a major role in helping the chemicals important for learning and memory move from one neuron to the next. The changes in NMDA are especially noticeable in the frontal cortex and the hippocampus, regions of the brain involved in declarative memories.

Another change that contributes to age-related memory loss is the development, starting around age sixty, of lesions in the brain's white matter, the bundles of axons that transmit messages throughout the brain and central nervous system. Psychologists in Scotland reported a unique longitudinal study in 2003 in which they compared the cognitive test scores of people at age seventy-eight with their test performance at age eleven. This comparison was possible because Scotland had conducted a survey of hundreds of eleven-year-olds in 1932 and kept the results on file in local health department offices. The tests assessed memory and learning, nonverbal reasoning, processing speed, and executive functions (the ability to plan ahead and coordinate different tasks).

MRI scanning of the brains of the seventy-eight-year-olds revealed that people with the most extensive white matter lesions exhibited the steepest decline in cognitive abilities relative to their performance as eleven-year-olds. Especially fascinating, the extent of white matter lesions was a slightly stronger predictor of test scores of people at age seventy-eight than their earlier scores were. You can see the difference in Figure 4.1, which shows a brain MRI of an elderly person with minimal white matter lesions and a brain MRI of a person of the same age with extensive white matter lesions.

We don't yet have a way to prevent white matter lesions from forming in old age, but we do know that these lesions are more common in some people than in others. People with cerebrovas-

FIGURE 4.1 White Matter

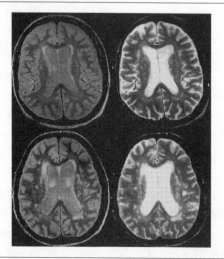

MRI of two age-matched (eighty-one-year-old) individuals, one with minimal white matter lesions (top two panels) and the other with extensive white matter lesions (bottom two panels). Lesions are present in the deep white matter surrounding the butterfly-shaped ventricles, appearing as light gray spots (on the left) and white spots (on the right). From C. R. Guttmann, R. Benson, S. K. Warfield et al., "White Matter Abnormalities in Mobility-Impaired Older Persons," Neurology, 54, 1277–1283. Reprinted by permission of Lippincott Williams & Wilkins.

cular risk factors, including hypertension, high cholesterol, heart disease, and diabetes, are especially prone to white matter disease. To the extent that you can reduce your risk of these diseases, you may also be able to minimize the accumulation of white matter lesions in the brain—and preserve your memory and related functions. (I discuss this in more detail in Chapter 5.)

The fact that some people age more successfully than others is not surprising, and there is evidence of variability in the way our brains change with age. In a 2002 study at Stanford University, fMRI was used to measure the pattern of brain activation in three subregions of the frontal cortex during a memory task in young adults and two subgroups of elderly people. The subgroup of elderly people with worse memory performance exhibited decreased levels of activation in all three brain regions compared to the group of elders who demonstrated better memory performance. When compared to their young counterparts, the high-performing elders exhibited a similar pattern of brain activation in two areas and greater activation in the third area. This finding suggests that the

Is Your Brain Shrinking?

Most people's brains do shrink, or atrophy, with age. But the number of lost neurons is relatively small. It turns out that the decrease in brain volume and mass in normal aging results not so much from an actual loss of neurons but rather from changes within neurons: loss of neuronal branches (dendritic spines), decreased density of synapses, and deterioration of the myelin sheath that surrounds the axons of neurons.

Only in the presence of memory disorders, such as Alzheimer's disease, does the brain suffer dramatic destruction and loss of neurons. Loss of neurons in the hippocampus and eventually other areas of the brain directly contributes to the pronounced difficulty with short-term memory that's typical of people with Alzheimer's disease.

more highly activated region in the brains of the elderly high performers was being recruited to help out with the mental work of the memory task. This functional recruitment may be one of the compensatory tactics employed by the successfully aging brain.

Which Cognitive Functions Are Most Vulnerable to Aging?

Age-related changes in the brain are likely to affect your memory and related operations in different ways. These functions are prone to age-related difficulties:

- **Working memory.** Your ability to hold and manipulate information in mind is reduced. Remembering a phone number and then dialing or comparing the price per ounce of two items are some examples.
- **Processing speed.** Speed of processing is slowed, which can affect retrieval of the names of acquaintances as well as your ability to keep pace in conversations or other communications that need to be processed on the spot. In fact, one major theory of age-related cognitive change, called the *processing speed theory*, argues that a general slowing of processing speed underlies all changes in cognitive function and memory. Slower processing leads to less effective and less complete encoding of information, which, in turn, results in weaker memory.
- **Attention to detail.** It's more of a challenge to perform tasks involving attention to detail. When you learn new information, you may take in the big picture, or gist, as well as someone half your age, but you might not absorb as many details. For instance, after looking at a painting for a minute, a twenty-five-year-old and a fifty-five-year-old might both remember that it depicted a landscape with a lot of greens and pinks, but the twenty-five-year-old will probably be able to remember more of the specific elements or features, such as the rabbits under a bush or a small canoe in the lake.

- **Declarative memory.** You have more trouble forming declarative memories. Specifically, you may find it harder to remember verbal facts (such as the names of people, places, and objects) and spatial information (such as the directions to a new location). You may also have more difficulty retrieving previously acquired declarative information (such as a specific word or name).

- **Source memory.** It becomes harder to recall when and where a specific event occurred, a type of memory referred to as source memory. You may remember parking your car, but you may not recall precisely where. Or you may remember a dinner at your favorite restaurant, but you may be unable to recall if you went there two months ago or four months ago.

- **Multitasking.** It becomes more difficult to multitask—that is, attend to more than one activity at a time. This is particularly distressing in an era where technological advances may put you in the position of juggling two or more tasks at once, like talking on the phone while working on the computer.

- **Visuospatial processing.** Complex visual and construction tasks, such as assembling three-dimensional puzzles and drawing intricate geometric designs, are more of a challenge.

Which Cognitive Functions Are Age-Resistant?

The changes that occur in the brain as you age might sound disturbing, but there are many domains of thinking that age doesn't touch. These resilient functions can help you overcome some of the age-related difficulties with learning and memory:

- **Attention.** The ability to focus and sustain attention is relatively unchanged by the aging process.
- **Language.** We retain a rich knowledge of words and word meanings as we age, and we maintain the ingrained rules for how to combine words into meaningful linguistic structures.

51

- **Procedural memory.** The skills and procedures for doing things (for instance, riding a bicycle or playing the piano) remain largely intact over the life span. The ability to form new procedural memories is also relatively well preserved.
- **Reasoning.** Aging has no effect on your ability to make sense of what you know, to form reasonable judgments, and to construct solid arguments.
- **Willpower.** Your drive to accomplish is undiminished by changes in the brain that are strictly age-related. Indeed, we now know that in many instances, if you have the will to make the extra effort to concentrate and learn something well, you will be rewarded—you will be able to recall it as well as a younger person can.
- **Creativity.** You retain the drive to express yourself through art, through communication, or by trying new ways of doing things.
- **Wisdom.** There's a reason that we often associate wisdom with advancing years: the capacity to extract meaning from information and knowledge from experience and to offer insights remains unscathed and may in fact improve with the passage of time. It should come as no surprise that the average age of the current justices of the U.S. Supreme Court is seventy and that their average age when appointed was about fifty.

Is There a Fountain of Youth for Your Brain?

We all know that some people age better than others. There are sixty-year-olds who are fit and trim and others who are lethargic and overweight. Some forty-five-year-olds have few wrinkles— and that's not just because of cosmetic surgery! Similarly, some people's brains remain relatively youthful.

To a large extent, how well you age depends on your genes. But a large number of factors are within your control. Just as you can reduce the number of wrinkles on your face by staying out of the sun, you can reduce some age-related changes in the brain with good habits, such as eating a healthy diet, getting regular physical exercise, and challenging your brain by learning new things.

Some of the same health habits that help protect the brain from the effects of age can also help prevent memory problems. In the next chapter, you'll learn about several reversible causes of memory difficulties and what you can do to control them.

CHAPTER 5

Causes of
Memory Problems

Michael was worried. His primary care physician referred him to me because he was concerned that he was developing Alzheimer's disease. He anxiously recounted, in minute detail, a half dozen instances of memory failure over the past few months, including a forgotten name, a missed appointment, and a wrong exit on the interstate.

As the consultation progressed, I asked a routine question regarding how he'd been faring emotionally. For Michael, this question triggered a pained expression, which darkened his face, and caused him to shift uncomfortably in his chair. He told me he'd been depressed for more than a year, since the death of his grandson in a car accident. Although he received spiritual counseling from his minister, he had not been able to shake the grief, which waited for him every time he sought sleep and each morning upon awakening. He had also become prone to awakening in the early hours of the morning, unable to resume sleep. He felt as if he had been dragging himself out of bed, beginning each day with a sense of exhaustion.

Michael had a neurological examination and a brain imaging study, both of which were normal. My clinical examination revealed the classic signs of depression with weak performance on measures of attention and concentration with mild secondary impairment on tests of new learning and memory.

Michael began psychotherapy to work through his grief over his grandson's death; he also started taking an antidepressant. His depression began to lift and his sleep improved; the medication was discontinued after five months. His neuropsychological examination was entirely normal at a six-month follow-up.

Like Michael, many patients with memory problems who come for evaluation discover that the cause is something that they never imagined could impair their ability to think and remember. Often, the cause is a common condition (such as depression) or a disorder that increases the risk of cerebrovascular disease and heart disease (such as poorly controlled high blood pressure or diabetes). Other causes of memory loss are hormonal changes that occur naturally during certain stages of life. For women, hormonal fluctuations following childbirth and around menopause can make them feel less sharp. Men also go through a phase of significant hormonal change as they age; a drop in testosterone level has been linked with age-related memory problems. Still other causes of memory loss are unhealthy habits (such as excessive alcohol use and getting too little exercise or sleep) or a lack of intellectual challenge.

Fortunately, many causes of memory dysfunction are preventable or treatable. You can consume less alcohol. You can eat sensibly and exercise regularly to reduce your risk of cardiovascular disease and diabetes, both of which can lead to cerebrovascular compromise and reduced blood flow to the brain. I give a complete description of these and other strategies in Chapter 9. In addition, treating underlying conditions that cause memory loss (such as hypertension) can help keep your memory in optimal condition.

Although you can change a multitude of factors that affect the quality of your memory, some causes of memory loss are beyond your control, such as your genetic background.

Genes

Dozens of studies involving more than ten thousand pairs of twins raised apart have shown that genetic differences account for about half of the variation in mental abilities. Genes help determine how your brain develops and evolves over your life span. Your genes affect how strong your memory is to begin with and how much it declines with age. And they affect your risk of many illnesses that impair memory, including Alzheimer's disease, hypertension, and depression.

Several genes related to Alzheimer's disease have been identified over the past ten years. It is certain that there are other as yet undiscovered genes and more complex gene interactions that play a major role in both normal memory function and predisposition to memory disorder. The details are fairly technical, but following is an outline of five genes that are important for memory:

- **Apolipoprotein (ApoE).** One variant of the ApoE gene, ApoE e4, is known as a susceptibility gene because it increases risk of sporadic or late-onset familial Alzheimer's disease, though it doesn't actually cause the disorder. The e4 variant, or *allele*, is also associated with higher absorption of cholesterol and increased incidence of coronary artery disease. The other two alleles of ApoE (e2 and e3) are not associated with elevated risk; in fact, the e2 allele conveys a reduced risk of Alzheimer's disease.
- **Presenilin 1 and presenilin 2.** Presenilin 1 and presenilin 2 cause early-onset familial Alzheimer's disease, a relatively rare form of the memory disorder that affects people younger than about sixty years old. In their mutated forms, these genes promote the production of the destructive plaques in the brain that are the key pathological feature of Alzheimer's. Presenilin 1 is the more common of the two genes, found in nearly half of people with early-onset Alzheimer's.

- **Amyloid precursor protein gene.** Mutations in this gene also cause early-onset Alzheimer's disease. Like the presenilin genes, mutation of the amyloid precursor protein gene results in increased production of the substance found in the destructive plaques that aggregate in the brains of people with Alzheimer's disease.

- **Brain-derived neurotropic factor (BDNF).** BDNF is a gene that directs the production of brain growth factor, a chemical that flows to the synapses, or spaces, between neurons to help relay messages. Although the connection between BDNF and Alzheimer's disease is not as well established as the other genes discussed here, people with the so-called met variant of BDNF have been found to have weaker episodic memory than people with another variant of the gene, called val, according to a 2003 study in the journal *Cell*. The brains of people with the met variant also appeared to operate abnormally. Functional MRI revealed that people with this gene variant had a different pattern of activity in the hippocampus than did people without the gene variant, a difference that probably accounts for their weaker episodic memory.

We have much more to learn about genes and Alzheimer's disease. In addition to the genetic mutations that cause Alzheimer's disease, it's certain that some genes exist that protect against the disease. Understanding what all these genes are and how they work is bound to bring us closer to being able to prevent and treat this disorder.

Hormones

Sex hormones definitely affect memory; this is true for men as well as women. With age, estrogen levels in women and testosterone levels in men fall, and this decline undoubtedly contributes to age-related memory loss.

Many women notice problems with memory during meno-pause, when their estrogen levels drop dramatically. It could be that estrogen benefits memory by protecting neurons, as some laboratory studies suggest. As for men, those with high levels of testosterone in their blood have better visual and verbal memory than men with low testosterone levels, according to a large study reported by the National Institute on Aging. Low testosterone may increase the risk of memory disorders. Men with low testos-terone were more likely to develop Alzheimer's disease in a study reported in the journal *Neurology* in 2004.

A logical question to ask is whether hormone supplements can help prevent age-related memory loss or Alzheimer's disease. For years, doctors thought that the answer was yes, at least for women. But that assumption was disproved by a large clinical trial, the Women's Health Initiative Memory Study (WHIMS).

Researchers from the WHIMS group reported in 2003 that combination estrogen–progestin therapy (Prempro) not only failed to improve memory in postmenopausal women but actually dou-bled the women's risk for dementia. Research in 2004 established that estrogen therapy by itself was also associated with an increased incidence of dementia. The Women's Health Initiative found that estrogen increased the risk of stroke in healthy women, and a related study found that it might also increase the risk of mild cognitive impairment, a condition that many experts con-sider to be a precursor of Alzheimer's disease.

Although all of the pieces of the estrogen puzzle are not yet in place as critics have questioned aspects of the WHIMS study design and resulting conclusions, menopausal hormone therapies now bear warning labels stating that they do not prevent memory loss and do slightly increase the risk of developing dementia.

The jury is still out on the benefit of testosterone supplemen-tation in men; we still don't know much about its long-term effects. A study in the *Journal of Cognitive Neuroscience* in 2000 found that men improved their working memory after taking testosterone supplements. But as with postmenopausal estrogen and estrogen-progestin replacement, testosterone therapy can increase the risk of certain types of cancers and has been linked to a higher incidence of stroke in some men. When I have a male patient with symptoms of low testosterone—decreased libido, lowered overall drive, general malaise—I recommend that he have his hormone levels checked by his primary care physician or an endocrine specialist. These doctors can knowledgeably discuss the pros and cons of testosterone treatment.

Common Age-Related Illnesses

Some illnesses that become more common with age can weaken memory, either directly or indirectly. The medications used to treat some of them can impair memory or concentration as well. (Alzheimer's disease, the most familiar age-related illness that causes memory loss, is listed under "Neurological Disorders" a little later in this chapter.)

Coronary Artery Disease and Its Risk Factors

What's bad for your heart is also bad for your brain. Conditions that are risk factors for cerebrovascular disease and heart disease, such as high cholesterol, hypertension, and diabetes, increase the risk of memory problems. Controlling these disorders with medication, dietary changes, and exercise can help keep your memory in optimal condition.

High Cholesterol. If your total cholesterol level is high, you're more likely to suffer memory problems in the years ahead than if the level is what doctors now consider optimal—less than 200 milligrams per deciliter (mg/dL), as shown in Table 5.1. Specifically, people with elevated cholesterol are at increased risk of a number of brain disorders, including mild cognitive impairment, stroke, and Alzheimer's disease.

We don't know exactly how high cholesterol leads to memory loss or whether the crucial factor is excessive low-density lipopro-

TABLE 5.1 Cholesterol and Triglyceride Levels

Total Cholesterol Level	Category
Less than 200 mg/dL	Desirable
200–239 mg/dL	Borderline high
240 mg/dL and above	High

LDL Cholesterol Level	Category
Less than 100 mg/dL	Optimal
100–129 mg/dL	Near/above optimal
130–159 mg/dL	Borderline high
160–189 mg/dL	High
190 mg/dL and above	Very high

HDL Cholesterol Level	Category
Less than 40 mg/dL	Low (representing increased risk)
60 mg/dL and above	High (heart-protective)

Triglyceride Level	Category
Less than 150 mg/dL	Normal
150–199 mg/dL	Borderline high
200–499 mg/dL	High
500 mg/dL and above	Very high

Adapted from National Heart, Lung, and Blood Institute, *Third Report of the National Cholesterol Education Program (NCEP) Expert Panel on Detection, Evaluation, and Treatment of High Blood Cholesterol in Adults (Adult Treatment Panel III) Final Report, May 2001, p. 13.*

teins (LDL, the "bad" cholesterol) or insufficient high–density lipoproteins (HDL, the "good" cholesterol). But there is some preliminary evidence from some recent studies that people with elevated cholesterol who are treated with statins, a class of cholesterol-lowering medications, may gain the additional benefit of decreasing their risk for Alzheimer's disease and mild cognitive impairment. More definitive studies are under way to determine the potential role of statins in the prevention and treatment of dementia.

Hypertension. Regardless of age, you're more prone to memory impairment if you have high blood pressure than if you have normal blood pressure. Moreover, your memory impairment is likely

Memory Loss Following Heart Surgery

More than 500,000 Americans undergo coronary artery bypass surgery each year for the treatment of angina and vascular insufficiency. People who've undergone bypass surgery for heart disease often have trouble concentrating and remembering. The exact cause of these cognitive problems is not clear, but there are probably many factors. They include the impact of anesthesia and major surgery, disruption of oxygen flow to the brain during the procedure, damage to blood vessels, and a generalized inflammatory response with increased permeability of the *blood-brain barrier* (a physiological mechanism that modifies capillaries, preventing certain substances from entering the brain). A crucial question is whether these troubling effects are temporary or permanent. A related question is, to what extent did these deficits exist prior to surgery?

In a report published in the *New England Journal of Medicine* in 2001, researchers at Duke University reported that 53 percent of coronary artery bypass surgery patients had cognitive deficits upon

to be more severe. You have hypertension if your systolic blood pressure (the pressure while the heart is beating) is consistently 140 mm Hg or higher or if your diastolic blood pressure (the pressure between beats) is consistently 90 mm Hg or higher.

We think that hypertension impairs memory by damaging tiny blood vessels that terminate in the brain's white matter, the bundles of axons that transmit messages throughout the brain and central nervous system. Lesions, or abnormalities, in white matter occur to some degree in virtually everyone older than age sixty and contribute to age-related memory loss. But people with hypertension have more extensive white matter damage than same-age peers with normal blood pressure.

Research suggests that hypertension that is inadequately treated might also predispose you to dementia. There's an additive effect;

discharge from the hospital. Although the incidence of cognitive problems declined to 24 percent after six months, the authors surprisingly found an increase in problems at a five-year follow-up, with 42 percent of cases exhibiting deficits. In contrast, a German research group included a strong postoperative management approach to control vascular risk factors and found overall neuropsychological *improvement* in their fifty-two patients at a follow-up in thirty-two to sixty-five months; no patient exhibited global cognitive decline.

Newer surgical methods, including an "off-pump" approach, appear to offer better cognitive outcomes. Long-term cognitive outcomes after bypass surgery will improve with future investigation of the use of neuroprotective agents before surgery, ongoing refinement of anesthesiologic and surgical techniques, and a strong commitment to management of vascular risk factors in the postsurgical phase.

brain imaging studies suggest that increased blood pressure can cause small strokes, which can then cause dementia. Hypertension also increases the risk for heart disease, which can cause memory loss. One common treatment for heart disease, coronary artery bypass surgery, can itself lead to memory impairment. (See the sidebar "Memory Loss Following Heart Surgery.")

The good news is that we think that lowering blood pressure may help preserve memory and other brain functions well into old age. So if you have hypertension, see your doctor and make sure it's adequately treated.

Diabetes. High blood sugar, the hallmark of diabetes, can impair the function of the hippocampus, the brain structure that consolidates declarative memories (for names, faces, dates, and other factual information). It's easy to understand why this happens. When sugar is elevated in the blood, it's not high enough in other parts of the body, including the brain. So the brain is low on fuel. Research has also demonstrated that diabetes can cause structural damage to the hippocampus and medial temporal lobes of the brain.

Memory problems are common among people with diabetes, as well as among people with mildly impaired glucose metabolism, whose blood sugar is slightly high. In 2003, researchers at New York University School of Medicine reported that people with suboptimal glucose metabolism achieved lower scores on short-term memory tests than people with normal blood sugar. What's more, the hippocampus was smaller in people with elevated blood sugar. Suboptimal glucose metabolism (also known as reduced glucose tolerance) is one of the five characteristics of Syndrome X, a collection of risk factors for heart disease that tend to aggregate in some people. The other factors are hypertension, elevated triglyceride, low HDL (good cholesterol), and abdominal obesity.

Evidence also suggests that people with diabetes mellitus (type 1 diabetes) may be at increased risk of developing Alzheimer's disease later in life. Again, the connection between diabetes and the risk of developing a memory disorder is almost certainly due to the link between diabetes and cerebrovascular disease. Although insulin injections, needed by many people who have type 1 diabetes, can cause mild memory impairment, this effect is typically seen only immediately after the medication is administered and usually resolves completely. So if you have either type 1 or type 2 diabetes, it's vital to get appropriate treatment not only to get your blood sugar under control but also to guard against possible further memory decline.

If your blood sugar is normal, take measures to keep it that way. Type 2 diabetes is primarily a disease of poor health habits: being sedentary and overweight. By maintaining normal weight and exercising regularly, you can prevent this disease and help keep your cognitive function in good shape. (For more information, see Chapter 9.)

Thyroid Dysfunction

The thyroid gland secretes hormones that control your metabolism, the rate at which your body burns energy. When the thyroid doesn't function properly, it can make your metabolism run too quickly or too slowly. Either problem can interfere with learning and memory. Research with animals demonstrates that changes in levels of thyroid hormones cause physiological changes in the hippocampus.

An overactive thyroid (hyperthyroidism) can impair your memory and your ability to sustain attention. Hyperthyroidism is also associated with anxiety, insomnia, and tremor. An underactive thyroid (hypothyroidism) can cause generalized cognitive slowing, sluggishness, and psychiatric symptoms. If you suffer from thyroid problems, getting the proper medical treatment should help prevent or diminish memory difficulties.

Neurological Disorders

Several neurological disorders cause direct damage to neurons and neuronal networks or prevent neurons from functioning properly, leading to memory loss and other types of cognitive dysfunction.

Alzheimer's Disease

Alzheimer's disease is undoubtedly—and with good reason—the most widely known neurological illness that causes memory loss. Alzheimer's disease is the leading cause of dementia, affecting an estimated four and a half million Americans at a cost of $100 billion per year, with the number of cases in the United States expected to reach between eleven and sixteen million by 2050.

Alzheimer's disease causes substantial loss of neurons along with the appearance of characteristic pathological features in the brain: *amyloid plaques* and *neurofibrillary tangles*. These plaques and tangles contain *beta-amyloid*, the "sticky" proteinaceous substance that is thought to be central to the Alzheimer's disease process. Early in the course of the disease, these features are concentrated in the hippocampus and cause the hallmark memory deficits. As the disease progresses, most areas of the cortex become involved, and cognitive function becomes globally affected. You'll learn more about Alzheimer's disease in Chapter 7 and about its treatment in Chapter 8.

Stroke

After Alzheimer's disease, the second leading cause of dementia is stroke. A stroke occurs when blood supply to part of the brain is interrupted. Neurons, like cells elsewhere in the body, require a continuous supply of blood-borne oxygen in order to function and remain viable. When blood flow to the brain is reduced or obstructed during a stroke, neurons are starved for nourishment and may die.

Even "silent" strokes—those that cause few or no observable symptoms—can cause dementia. A large study published in the *New England Journal of Medicine* in 2003 found that people who had silent strokes were more than twice as likely to develop dementia within three and a half years compared with people who did not have silent strokes. Even those who didn't develop dementia exhibited a sharper decline in performance on memory tests and overall intellectual functioning compared with people who did not have strokes.

Stroke may act synergistically with underlying Alzheimer's pathology to produce clinical disease. In a widely publicized study of aging nuns, researchers at the University of Kentucky reported in the *Journal of the American Medical Association (JAMA)* in 1997 that participants who had sustained stroke were much more likely to have a diagnosis of dementia than their counterparts who had an equivalent degree of plaque and tangle pathology in their brains but who had not had a stroke. In other words, a stroke, in many cases quite small, lowered the amount of Alzheimer's pathology necessary to cause symptoms of dementia.

Hypertension, hypercholesterolemia (high cholesterol), and diabetes increase your risk for stroke. Although genetic heritage has a lot to do with your likelihood of developing these diseases, lifestyle factors and behaviors are at least as important. You can reduce your risk of these illnesses by avoiding smoking, eating a healthy diet, maintaining a normal weight, and being physically active on a regular basis. If you have hypertension or high cholesterol, make sure you get it under control with a combination of appropriate treatment and improved lifestyle choices and habits.

Head Trauma

A blow to the head that's severe enough to cause a concussion (a brief impairment of consciousness) can temporarily impair your memory. The impact can directly damage brain cells. It can also stretch or tear the axons, the fine "tails" of neurons that compose the white matter, the communication system of the brain and spinal cord.

Most people who suffer a mild concussion recover their memory and other brain functions completely within a few hours or days. But severe head trauma, such as an injury from a high-speed motor vehicle accident, often causes permanent damage. In addition, people who've incurred repeated minor concussions (for example, professional boxers) are prone to developing dementia and other brain disorders later in life. Years of playing competitive contact sports that involve repeated blows to the head, such as soccer or ice hockey, can exact a toll on memory and related brain functions in later life.

The issue of concussion in both recreational and professional sports has been gaining increasing exposure over the past decade. In fact, many professional teams have adopted guidelines for management of concussion and return to play. In 1997, the National Hockey League instituted a concussion management program in which every player who enters the league undergoes a standardized neuropsychological screening. Test data from screening is used as a baseline in the event of a future concussion. Each team has a designated neuropsychologist who examines players in the aftermath of concussion and assists in return-to-play decisions. I serve in this capacity for the Boston Bruins.

There has been a corresponding ripple effect through hundreds of universities and secondary school systems in the United States with regard to a wide range of contact sports. You can reduce your risk of concussive injury and head trauma by wearing a seat belt whenever you're in a car and by using protective headgear for activities such as bicycling, motorcycling, in-line skating, skiing, snowboarding, and contact sports.

Parkinson's Disease

Though tremor and other problems with movement are the main features of Parkinson's disease, one-third to one-half of the one million Americans with Parkinson's also have significant cognitive and memory problems. Parkinson's disease, which is most common in people over the age of fifty, involves the loss of neurons in a brain structure called the substantia nigra, which produces *dopamine*, a chemical messenger that controls movement and helps you form memories. Patients with Parkinson's disease frequently exhibit deficits on tasks of visuospatial analysis and construction (such as assembling puzzles and designs). A small subset of patients develop global dementia with severe deficits in multiple cognitive domains, including memory.

Though the disease is chronic and has no cure, there are medications that can relieve the movement symptoms by providing dopamine. The motor response to medication does not necessarily predict the cognitive response. Surgery and brain stimulation techniques have been developed for treatment of some patients for whom medication does not adequately control the movement disorder.

Lewy-Body Disease

Lewy bodies are hallmark pathological features found in the neurons of people with Parkinson's disease. They also appear to play a role in other neurodegenerative disorders that cause dementia. Cortical Lewy-body disease refers to a dementia that presents with Parkinsonian motor symptoms (primarily rigidity and gait disorder), as well as fluctuating attention and alertness, visual hallucinations, delusional thinking, and other psychiatric and behavioral features.

The primary initial neuropsychological findings are found in the realms of attention and high-order visual processing, such as analysis of complex images and the ability to draw designs and assemble puzzles. Although performance on memory testing is rarely normal, memory impairment is not the most prominent cognitive finding, particularly in the early phase. The relationship between Lewy bodies and dementia is not yet clear, and the overlap with Alzheimer's disease has made reliable diagnosis of this disorder difficult and somewhat controversial. One school of thought is that most people with Lewy-body dementia also have Alzheimer's disease.

Multiple Sclerosis

This progressive disease destroys *myelin*, the sheath that normally protects neuronal axons, which constitute the white matter of the brain and spinal cord. The result is that electrical impulses from neurons are either slow to reach their targets or fail to arrive altogether. Neurons can also become damaged, further interfering with neuronal communication. Depending on where in the nervous system this damage occurs, it can impair any neurological function, including memory, sensation, and the control of movement. The most common neurological symptoms include numbness, weakness, and paralysis.

About half of people with multiple sclerosis have cognitive difficulties. As with physical symptoms, individual experiences with these symptoms differ considerably. The most common cognitive problems occur in the realms of attention, concentration, and executive functions, which refer to high-level cognitive functions, such as planning and reasoning. Deficits in these areas can have secondary impact on memory. In some people, these problems worsen over time, whereas in others, they remain stable or might even improve.

There's no cure for multiple sclerosis, but research indicates that certain medications can slow the progression of the disease.

Many people with MS-related cognitive symptoms respond well to medications that augment attention and alertness.

Epilepsy

This brain disorder is marked by recurrent seizures caused by abnormal brain electrical activity. It is difficult to estimate the prevalence of cognitive and memory problems in people with epilepsy because these problems can be caused by a large number of factors, including the illness itself, underlying brain pathology, antiepileptic medications, and epilepsy surgery. Regardless of the specific cause, cognitive symptoms are invariably at the top of the list of concerns presented by these patients.

In particular, verbal memory loss (difficulty remembering words) is a risk of temporal lobe epilepsy surgery, which is sometimes performed to control seizures when medication has not been effective. The risk is greatest with surgery in the left hemisphere, the side of the brain that is specialized for language in most people. Careful presurgical evaluation and planning can mitigate this risk for a large majority of patients. The strategies for optimal memory that I discuss in this book can be effective for people with epilepsy.

Lyme Disease

Lyme disease is the most common tick-borne illness in the United States, affecting an estimated fifteen thousand Americans each year. Common symptoms usually include joint pain and fatigue. Untreated, Lyme disease can eventually involve the central nervous system and cause deficits in attention, memory, speed of processing, and executive function.

Treatment of Lyme disease with antibiotics in the early acute phase usually results in symptom remission and cure. However, if the tick-borne spirochete enters the bloodstream and disseminates in other organ systems, intravenous antibiotics are usually necessary for definitive treatment. In exceedingly rare cases, the disease can result in persisting cognitive symptoms. When this happens, an intensive evaluation including spinal tap and cerebrospinal fluid analysis is needed to support the diagnosis.

Other Neurological Illnesses

Any illness that affects the brain can also impair memory. Less common neurological illnesses include encephalitis (an inflammation of the brain caused by a virus or microorganism), normal pressure hydrocephalus (an excess of cerebrospinal fluid in the ventricles of the brain), Huntington's disease (a genetically transmitted degenerative brain disorder), meningitis (an inflammation of the membranes surrounding the brain and spinal cord), and primary and metastatic brain tumors. These conditions are usually diagnosed quickly, as the initial symptoms are readily recognizable.

Cancer

Chemotherapy and radiation treatments for cancer can also induce memory loss. Researchers from M. D. Anderson Cancer Center in Houston recently assessed memory and other cognitive functions in women with breast cancer before and during chemotherapy. The study, published in the journal *Cancer* in 2004, found that 33 percent of the women had deficits in one or more of the following areas—learning and memory, processing speed, attention, and visual perception—before starting chemotherapy and that 61 percent had impairments within six months after starting chemotherapy. Cognitive problems caused by chemotherapy are often transient; half of the women who experienced them in the M. D. Anderson study found that their deficits improved one year after treatment ended.

Radiation is used in the treatment of primary and metastatic brain tumors as well as prophylaxis against potential metastatic brain disease from cancers elsewhere in the body. In addition to destroying cancer cells, radiation can damage normal brain tissue either directly or by harming the tiny blood vessels that terminate in the white matter. Cognitive and memory problems can develop acutely or in delayed fashion, months or even years after treatment. Newer treatment techniques, including stereotactic radiation therapy, charged particle beam, and gamma knife methods, have significantly reduced these types of adverse side effects by more precisely targeting treatment and dividing radiation dosage over time.

In addition to primary brain tumors and cancer treatment effects, cancers elsewhere in the body can impair memory, attention, and speed of processing. A *paraneoplastic syndrome* is a rare neurological disorder triggered by the immune system's response to cancer anywhere in the body. There are a number of distinctive syndrome subtypes, each producing a characteristic group of symptoms.

In these syndromes, antibodies against cancer mistakenly attack normal cells in the nervous system and cause striking neurological symptoms, often before the underlying cancer has been detected and diagnosed. Paraneoplastic syndromes are most common with cancers of the breast, ovary, lung, and lymphatic system. In addition to memory loss, paraneoplastic syndromes can cause problems with vision, swallowing, speech articulation, and walking, as well as profound weakness, seizures, and a range of other physical symptoms.

Mood, Stress, and Memory

Psychological disorders, such as depression and post-traumatic stress disorder, as well as significant stress, can interfere with optimal memory. Getting these problems under control usually restores memory function.

Depression
Depression can make it difficult to concentrate, focus on details, and absorb new information. And, as was the case with Michael, whom you met at the beginning of this chapter, depression can interfere with sleep, and sleep deprivation can compound cognitive problems. Research suggests that long-term depression can

even lead to a loss of neurons in the hippocampus and amygdala, structures that are important for memory. One study found that these structures were smaller in women with a history of recurrent depression than in women who didn't suffer from depression. In this study, the women with a history of depression performed poorly on verbal memory tests.

Treating depression leads to improvement in memory and other cognitive functions, often within a few months. Michael's experience was fairly typical. The combination of psychotherapy and medication for his depression and sleep disturbance successfully treated these problems and led to the full return of his cognitive function within six months.

In elderly people with severe depression, cognitive symptoms can occasionally be difficult to distinguish from a neurologically based dementia, such as Alzheimer's disease. In fact, the term *depressive pseudodementia* was coined to refer to this clinical presentation. Depression might also increase the risk of having Alzheimer's disease. But the relationship between depression and Alzheimer's disease is complex; depression can also be an early symptom of this disease. A study in the *Archives of Neurology* in 2003 found that a history of depression was more common among a group of 1,953 patients with Alzheimer's disease than it was among their relatives without Alzheimer's disease.

There are key differences in the memory loss experienced by people with depression alone versus the memory loss of people with depression and Alzheimer's disease. In people with depression alone, memory and other cognitive functions fluctuate with mood. When mood improves—usually in response to treatment with medication, psychotherapy, or both—cognitive function generally improves, too. In people with Alzheimer's disease and depression, memory and other mental functions don't improve when the depression lifts.

Post-Traumatic Stress Disorder (PTSD)

Some people who experience severe psychological trauma develop post-traumatic stress disorder, a condition characterized by recurring, intrusive memories of the traumatic event. These memories are highly persistent and interfere with the process of acquiring new information, consolidating memories, and remembering information that is unrelated to the trauma. Sustained levels of stress stimulate the release of a hormone called *cortisol*, which can ultimately damage brain structures that are important for memory. In fact, patients with PTSD have been found to have structural changes in the hippocampus and possibly other areas of the limbic system.

High levels of cortisol can also cause memory problems in people without PTSD. In one study, healthy adults were given a supplemental dose of cortisol once a day for four days. The people were divided into two groups. One group was given a low dose of cortisol—about the level that the body naturally releases in response to ordinary stressful events, such as getting stuck in traffic and being late for an appointment. The other group received a high dose of cortisol. All participants took a test in which they listened to stories and then had to remember details about them immediately and again thirty minutes later. The people who received the high cortisol dose remembered less, both immediately and later, than did the people receiving the lower dose.

The memory problems induced by this four-day experiment were reversible; once the cortisol wore off, the participants' memory function returned to normal. In like manner, research shows that timely and effective treatment of PTSD can improve memory function. However, memory deficits will persist if there has been structural damage to the hippocampus or other parts of the limbic system.

Stress

Try to memorize a phone number or remember what someone just told you when you're in a time crunch or consumed with worry. Of course, we're all under stress. If you're working and raising a family, you have to juggle deadline pressures and office politics along with homework, soccer games, teenagers' social schedules, and so on. Financial problems are also a major source of stress for many people. If you have an ailing parent, the stress of caregiving adds to the mix.

Patients often ask me, "How much stress is too much?" I tell them that the answer depends less on the amount of stress they have than on their response to it.

We each deal with stress differently. Some people work long hours at high-pressure jobs but remain focused and composed. Others in this situation become overwhelmed. It's the *reaction to stress* that does the damage.

As I mentioned before, an intense stress response triggers a surge in cortisol release, which can interfere with memory. Although short-term effects are reversible, we do not know how many days, weeks, months, or years of high-level stress it takes to cause persisting memory impairment.

You can control the harm that stress does to your memory by finding ways to modify your response to stressful life events. Vigorous physical activity helps some people overcome stress; others use meditation or relaxation techniques. For some, it's a matter of learning their limits—how much stress they can take on—and developing assertiveness in politely but firmly declining a task or commitment. Everyone's different. What's important is that you find stress-management activities that are effective for you. I discuss scientifically proven stress-reduction techniques in Chapter 9.

Memory Myth: All Stress Is Bad

Excessive stress can blunt your memory, but a modest amount of stress can actually sharpen it. The pressure of a looming deadline may increase your ability to focus and sustain attention. The result is that you acquire information more effectively, which in turn promotes memory consolidation and retrieval. Without some sense of urgency, your focus is likely to blur, resulting in diminished assimilation of information and ineffective memory consolidation.

But a word of advice. Don't run away from stress entirely. Too little stress can actually undermine memory function. Have you ever spent a week on the beach only to wonder what day it is? That's because there's no urgency to concentrate or recall information. That carefree feeling is fine for vacation, but imagine what your life would be like if you had so little pressure year-round? Chances are, your cognitive function would go "on vacation," too—and imagine how stressed out that would make you feel! A modest amount of stress puts you on alert, sharpens your attentional focus, and prepares you to learn.

Medications

If your memory declines after starting a new medication, there could well be a connection. Many prescription drugs can impair memory, as you can see in Table 5.2. The effects tend to come on fairly suddenly—usually within days or weeks of starting a medication.

Many medications require an initial phase of adaptation during which there may be a range of side effects. Your doctor may make adjustments in your dose or medication-taking schedule to help you through this phase. In many cases, side effects are transient and will resolve in short order. In some cases, however, unacceptable cognitive side effects persist and necessitate switching to an alternative medication.

Any medication that makes you drowsy can impair your memory by making it difficult to concentrate. Such medications include tranquilizers, sleeping pills, and certain antihistamines. Anticholinergic agents, such as those used to treat Parkinson's disease or urinary incontinence, block the activity of *acetylcholine*, a neurotransmitter that is crucial for memory. The tricyclic class of antidepressants also has potent anticholinergic side effects. Other medicines that can cause memory dysfunction include narcotic painkillers (such as morphine or oxycodone), beta-blockers for hypertension, cimetidine (Tagamet) for ulcers, benzodiazepines

TABLE 5.2 Medications* and Memory Loss

Class of Drug	Generic Name	Brand Name
Sleeping medications	estazolam	ProSom
	flurazepam	Dalmane
	temazepam	Restoril
	triazolam	Halcion
	zaleplon	Sonata
	zolpidem	Ambien
Tranquilizers/anxiety medications	alprazolam	Xanax
	buspirone	BuSpar
	clorazepate	Tranxene
	diazepam	Valium
	lorazepam	Ativan
	meprobamate	Equanil, Miltown
	oxazepam	Serax
Pain medications	meperidine	Demerol
	tramadol and acetaminophen	Ultracet
	tramadol	Ultram
Antihypertensives	methyldopa	Aldomet
	propranolol	Inderal
Heartburn medications	cimetidine	Tagamet
Antidepressants	amoxapine	Asendin
	amitriptyline	
	citalopram	Celexa
	desipramine	Norpramin
	imipramine	Tofranil
	nortriptyline	Pamelor, Aventyl HCl
	paroxetine	Paxil
Antiepileptics	clonazepam	Klonopin
	divalproex sodium	Depakote
	gabapentin	Neurontin
	lamotrigine	Lamictal
	levetiracetam	Keppra
	oxcarbazepine	Trileptal
	phenytoin	Dilantin
	phenobarbital	
	topiramate	Topamax
	zonisamide	Zonegran

continued

TABLE 5.2 Medications* and Memory Loss, *continued*

Class of Drug	Generic Name	Brand Name
Antipsychotics	chlorpromazine	Thorazine
	haloperidol	Haldol
	olanzapine	Zyprexa
	risperidone	Risperdal
	thioridazine	Mellaril
Parkinson's disease medications	amantadine	Symmetrel
	benztropine	Cogentin
	levodopa	
	levodopa and carbidopa	Sinemet
	pramipexole	Mirapex
	ropinirole	Requip
	selegiline	Eldepryl
	trihexyphenidyl	Artane
Anticholinergics (to treat tremor or urinary incontinence)	oxybutynin	Ditropan
	tolterodine	Detrol
Antinausea medications	dronabinol	Marinol
Antimania medications	lithium	Eskalith, Lithobid

*Common prescription drugs that may cause transient memory loss as a side effect

for anxiety, amantadine (Symmetrel) for Parkinson's disease, and various forms of cancer chemotherapy.

As you age, you're more prone to experience side effects from medications for three reasons. First, your metabolism slows down, which means that it takes your body longer to break down and absorb medications. Second, you are more likely to be taking several medications simultaneously—the more drugs you take, the greater the chance of an adverse reaction or a drug-drug interaction. Third, normal age-related changes in brain mass and functional capability effectively lower your threshold for contending with neurochemical effects.

If you are having memory problems and suspect that a medication is the culprit, make a list of all the medications you take regularly and review them with your doctor. Don't discontinue a medication unless your doctor says it's OK; otherwise, you might do more harm than good. Under your doctor's guidance, however, you might be able to stop taking a drug for a while to see whether your memory improves. It can take up to several weeks before you see any change. Your doctor might be able to replace an offending medication with a different drug that is better tolerated.

Sleep

People who sleep poorly at night tend to be more forgetful than people who sleep soundly. A good night's sleep is essential for memory consolidation. Although people vary in their need for sleep, six hours seems to be the minimum requirement to ensure that you are alert enough during the day to maintain optimal memory.

A 2000 Harvard study suggests that sleep improves skill learning. The skill, in this case, was performance on a visual discrimination task entailing rapid recognition of a subtle change in a visual pattern. The researchers found that college students who slept at least six hours performed better on the day following the initial learning than those who slept less than six hours. Students who slept eight hours did the best of all.

We believe that sleep benefits memory by enabling the brain to "replay" information that was encountered earlier. Evidence comes from imaging research in which researchers studied brain activity during memory acquisition and during a subsequent sleep phase. The scientists found that the neural pathways that were active during the learning period were reactivated during sleep. We believe that this is memory consolidation at work—that reactivation strengthens the neural pathways that hold the new information.

Sleep may also indirectly benefit memory by decreasing levels of stress hormones. As I mentioned earlier, stress hormones can interfere with memory by damaging the hippocampus. Stress hormones decline during the first few hours of sleep. Experts think that this decline helps the hippocampus operate at peak performance as it goes about its task of consolidating memories.

Insomnia

Staying up late of your own free will is one thing. But what if you're trying to get a good night's sleep and can't? Insomnia takes different forms. *Onset insomnia* refers to difficulty establishing sleep; common causes include anxiety and racing thoughts. *Middle insomnia* refers to middle-of-the-night awakening and an inability to return to sleep within a reasonable time. This type of problem is typical of people experiencing chronic pain, which may rouse them from the midst of slumber. Early morning awakening is frequently associated with depression. Whatever form insomnia takes, the net effect is the same: insufficient restorative sleep leading to daytime fatigue.

The detrimental effect of insomnia on memory function is twofold. Decreased sleep deprives you of adequate time for consolidation and diminishes daytime alertness, thereby undermining attentional function and new learning. All forms of insomnia become more common with age.

Occasional sleeplessness is common and does not require treatment. Feelings of excitement or apprehension (or both) the night before a big event may keep you awake. However, when sleep becomes regularly elusive, daytime functioning suffers. Insomnia can be both a cause and a symptom of depression.

Treatment of insomnia depends on the underlying cause and can include changing behaviors, the use of medication, or other medical procedures. Most sleep experts recommend beginning with a review of sleep hygiene, or presleep behaviors and other factors that influence sleep onset and maintenance, such as eating, ingesting alcohol or caffeine, and engaging in strenuous exercise in the hours prior to bedtime. Another important factor is maintaining a regular bedtime. If you go to bed very late one night, you'll find it more difficult to fall asleep at your normal bedtime the next night for the simple reason that you won't be tired enough.

Unfortunately, many medicines used to treat insomnia can also undermine memory. I advise patients to avoid long-term use of these sleep-aid drugs and instead to emphasize nonpharmacological approaches whenever possible. Meditative self-relaxation techniques are highly effective for many people. I discuss specific strategies for combating insomnia in Chapter 9.

Obstructive Sleep Apnea (OSA)

OSA is another disorder that degrades sleep quality and leads to impairment in daytime cognitive function. *Obstructive sleep apnea* refers to frequent interruptions of breathing caused by blockage of the upper airway. Respiratory interruptions result in transient lowering of blood oxygen levels, causing reflexive partial awakening in order to reestablish respiration.

In people with significant OSA, these disruptions can occur hundreds of times throughout the night and result in fragmentation of normal brain electrical activity and sleep architecture. OSA is usually caused by changes in airway anatomy, frequently associated with weight gain. Loud snoring and occasional gasping are near universal.

There are several treatments for OSA. Weight loss can eliminate the disorder. Some patients respond well to inhalers, which can open breathing passages. When these measures are not effective, doctors often recommend use of a c-pap (continuous positive airway pressure) device to keep the airways open during sleep. Although c-pap is an unequivocally effective treatment for OSA, many patients have difficulty tolerating the face mask, which is part of the device. An increasingly popular treatment alternative is upper airway laser surgery, which reshapes the tissues of the breathing passages. However, because surgery is less effective and much more invasive, an unstinting attempt at c-pap should precede surgical intervention.

People with effectively treated OSA consistently describe a rediscovered sense of rejuvenation, awakening refreshed and energized in a way they didn't believe was possible. They are less prone to depression and anxiety; although findings have been mixed, some studies report that cognitive function and memory performance are also improved.

Diet and Nutrition

Contrary to what you may have read on the Internet, there is no magic "brain food" to sharpen your memory. But we know that a poor diet is bad for your memory and that there are certain healthy foods and nutrients that just might help prevent memory loss.

B Vitamins

A strong link in the diet-memory connection seems to be with the B vitamins: folic acid and vitamins B_6 and B_{12}. These vitamins are not naturally produced within the body and must be obtained from food or supplements. B-complex vitamins are found in brewer's yeast, liver, whole-grain cereals, rice, nuts, milk, eggs, meats, fish, fruits, leafy green vegetables, and other foods. People with deficiencies in some or all of these vitamins are at greater risk of age-related memory impairment as well as dementia. Your daily intake of these nutrients should be 400 micrograms of folic acid, 1.3 to 1.7 milligrams of vitamin B_6, and 6 micrograms of vitamin B_{12}. But be careful with B_6 supplementation because excessive amounts can cause a peripheral neuropathy (numbness and tingling in the fingers and toes).

Vitamin B_{12} keeps neurons healthy by helping to make and preserve myelin, the fatty sheath that surrounds and protects axons. A deficiency of vitamin B_{12} can cause permanent damage to neurons, leading to memory loss, as well as slowing down your thinking and making you feel fatigued. Vitamin B_{12} deficiency becomes more common with age. Smoking and drinking also increase the risk of this vitamin deficiency.

Fortunately, vitamin B_{12} deficiency is easy to detect with a blood test and easy to correct with monthly injections of the vitamin. The injections can help prevent further memory impairment, but they often won't restore what's been lost. In most cases, it doesn't help to take vitamin B_{12} supplements orally if you have a deficiency because the most common cause is malabsorption, an inability to absorb the vitamin via the digestive process.

The Homocysteine Link. Another, more complex link in the connection between the B vitamins and memory loss has to do with homocysteine, an amino acid in the blood that's been getting a lot of attention lately.

Several years ago, evidence began mounting that a high level of homocysteine was a major risk factor for heart disease, stroke, and peripheral vascular disease. Then came evidence that a high homocysteine level was toxic to neurons and a strong risk factor for Alzheimer's disease and other forms of dementia. One cause of elevated homocysteine is a deficiency in folic acid and vitamins B_6 and B_{12}, which normally assist in the breakdown of homocysteine in the blood.

Your doctor can measure your homocysteine level with a blood test. Testing is particularly indicated for people at risk for stroke or heart attack, such as those with a personal or familial history of cardiovascular disease. Though there is no official cutoff level, research suggests that readings below 12 micromoles per liter are desirable. In a study in the *Annals of Neurology* in 2003, the risk of cognitive decline over the course of three years was nearly threefold among adults with homocysteine levels above 15 compared with people with lower levels.

We know that getting the recommended amounts of B vitamins, either through a healthy diet or supplements, can lower homocysteine levels. Keeping homocysteine low can probably help protect you against cognitive decline. What remains to be seen is whether increasing your intake of B vitamins can stabilize or reverse cognitive decline.

Good Fats, Bad Fats

For years, scientists regarded fat in the diet as universally bad for your brain. But we now know that only some fats are bad for your memory, whereas others are actually beneficial. Your brain can suffer under the influence of saturated fats (found mainly in meat and dairy products) and trans fats (found mostly in processed foods with partially hydrogenated oils). But your brain can thrive on unsaturated fats, which come from nuts, most vegetable oils, and fish oils.

A report in the *Archives of Neurology* in 2003 revealed that large amounts of saturated fats and trans fats were associated with an increased risk of Alzheimer's disease, whereas eating large amounts of unsaturated fats decreased risk. The study included a random sample of 815 people ages sixty-five and older with normal cognitive function. After four years, people who consumed the most saturated fat or trans fats were approximately twice as likely to develop Alzheimer's disease as were people who consumed the lowest amounts of these fats. In contrast, polyunsaturated fats and monounsaturated fats appeared to convey a protective benefit; risk of Alzheimer's disease was 70 percent lower among people who ate the most polyunsaturated fats compared with those who ate the least.

The same researchers also reported that eating fish regularly was protective for memory function. Study participants who ate fish once a week or more were 60 percent less likely to develop Alzheimer's disease than those who didn't eat fish. Fish is high in a type of polyunsaturated fat known as omega-3 fatty acids, which we think might improve nerve function as well as heart health.

It stands to reason that saturated fat is bad for your memory and unsaturated fats are beneficial. Saturated fat contributes to heart disease, hypertension, and high cholesterol, each of which increases the risk of age-related memory loss. Unsaturated fats are known to protect against these cardiovascular disorders. And we know that what's good for your heart is also good for your brain.

Antioxidants

Antioxidants (vitamins C and E and beta-carotene) neutralize destructive molecules called *free radicals*, which our bodies produce in large amounts as by-products of normal functioning. Because free radicals are prime suspects in many of the diseases and impairments that come with age, including dementia, scientists have long suspected that antioxidants might offer protection against memory loss. The newest research suggests that some antioxidants do indeed prevent age-related memory loss, as well as some forms of dementia.

A large study suggested that vitamin E, but not the other antioxidants, might help slow the rate of age-related mental decline. This study, published in the *Archives of Neurology* in 2002, looked at 2,889 people ages sixty-five and older who, at the outset, had normal memory and cognitive function. Researchers collected detailed nutritional profiles and asked the people which vitamin and mineral supplements they took, and then tracked their cognitive function over an average follow-up interval of three years. Cognitive function was measured using standard tests of attention and memory. The data revealed that people who consumed the most vitamin E exhibited 36 percent less mental decline during the course of the study than did people who consumed the least. It did not seem to matter whether vitamin E was obtained from regular food sources or supplements.

An earlier study had found that vitamins C and E might protect against some forms of dementia, though not Alzheimer's. In this study, which included 3,385 Japanese American men ages seventy-one to ninety-three, those who reported taking vitamin C and E supplements had an 88 percent lower incidence of vascular dementia (which is related to stroke) compared with men who didn't take the supplements. The rate of dementia was lowest among men who'd taken the vitamins the longest, suggesting that long-term use of these vitamins is important for helping to preserve mental function with aging.

In its latest guidelines on vitamin E supplementation, the National Academy of Science's Institute of Medicine set 1,000 IU per day as the upper limit that would be unlikely to cause side effects. However, researchers from Johns Hopkins reported in November 2004 that use of vitamin E supplements in excess of 400 IU per day were associated with a marginally higher degree of mortality. Although we must heed this finding, the study leaves many questions unanswered. More research will be necessary before we can make a final determination regarding recommended use of vitamin E.

You should discuss use of these supplements with your doctor. Vitamin E can affect platelet function and promote bleeding. High doses of vitamin E can be dangerous if you are taking medicine that decreases blood coagulation or if you have a bleeding disorder, such as hemophilia, thrombocytopenia, or von Willebrand's disease.

Alcohol

Like stress, alcohol in moderation can be good for your memory. Research has found that light-to-moderate alcohol use appears to reduce the risk of dementia. In a study published in the *Journal of the American Medical Association* in 2003, people over age sixty-five who consumed up to one drink a day had roughly half the risk of developing Alzheimer's disease compared with people who didn't drink at all. Heavy drinkers, on the other hand, had a 22 percent higher risk than did nondrinkers.

Excessive alcohol consumption inflicts damage in two ways: through direct toxic effects on neurons and by causing a deficiency of vitamin B_1 (thiamine). Thiamine deficiency can cause

Memory Myth: Alcohol Destroys Memory

Large amounts of alcohol are toxic to the brain, but small amounts appear to be beneficial. In recent studies, people who consumed alcohol in moderation had a reduced rate of Alzheimer's disease compared with people who did not drink at all. The exact mechanism of alcohol's beneficial effect is uncertain. One hypothesis is that alcohol reduces cardiovascular risk factors by altering blood lipids. Another hypothesis is that alcohol stimulates the release of the neurotransmitter acetylcholine in the hippocampus.

This doesn't mean that you should start drinking if you're opposed to using alcohol; there are many other ways to protect your memory. But if you do drink, holding your alcohol intake to one or two beverages per day could keep your brain healthy.

Korsakoff's syndrome, a disorder marked by sudden, dramatic (and usually permanent) memory loss. Apart from Korsakoff's syndrome, other alcohol-related memory problems are potentially treatable and, in some cases, reversible. Cessation of drinking, maintenance of adequate nutrition, and replenishment of vitamin B_1, if necessary, are the keys to treatment of alcohol-related memory dysfunction.

I advise patients to limit their use of alcohol; one or two drinks a day seems to be a sensible amount for protecting memory and optimizing other health concerns. In terms of alcohol equivalency, one drink equals twelve ounces of beer, five ounces of wine, or one and a half ounces of distilled spirits. This doesn't mean that nondrinkers should start drinking, but this benefit is worth noting if you do drink alcohol.

Exercise

My patients are surprised when I ask them if they exercise regularly. "What does that have to do with memory?" they ask. A lot, it turns out.

A landmark study conducted in the 1980s and 1990s—the MacArthur Foundation Study of Aging in America—found that sedentary people exhibited greater memory decline than people who engaged in regular physical activity. The active people didn't necessarily work out at a gym, but they did build more activity into their daily schedule. They went for walks almost every day or climbed stairs at home.

We don't know exactly why physical fitness influences brain fitness, but there are a few possible explanations. The most intriguing possibility is that physical activity increases levels of beneficial brain chemicals. In a MacArthur laboratory study, rats that were most active had the highest levels of nerve growth factor, a substance also found in the human brain that helps maintain neurons and repair them after injury. If exercise has the same beneficial effect for us, then it could be one of the best methods we have to keep our neurons in good shape.

Exercise might also benefit memory indirectly by keeping the lungs and the cardiovascular system healthy and delivering a steady supply of oxygen to the brain. The MacArthur researchers found that good lung function was one characteristic of elderly individuals who had the strongest memory and overall cognitive function. As for cardiovascular health, it's well established that regular exercise reduces the risk of hypertension, high cholesterol, and heart disease and that, in people who have these conditions, exercising helps keep them under control. Once again, what's good for your heart is also good for your brain.

A 2004 University of Illinois study found that people with high levels of aerobic fitness exhibited greater activation in key brain regions during performance of cognitive tasks as compared with their less fit counterparts. The researchers speculated that cardiovascular fitness leads to increased density of synapses and increased blood flow to active brain regions. All of these effects would be beneficial for brain function and the mitigation of typical aging effects.

So if you don't currently exercise regularly, find ways to be more physically active. Aim for at least thirty minutes of vigorous activity each day, by walking, biking, or doing whatever kind of exercise you enjoy. I describe specific strategies for getting started and finding time to exercise in Chapter 9.

Intellectual Stimulation

If ever there was a reason to turn off the sitcom reruns and read a book, it's this: there's a connection between how much you use your brain and how well it performs as you age. Over time, people who challenge their minds maintain a greater degree of memory resiliency than people who are mentally disengaged.

The MacArthur study found that *the strongest predictor* of mental capacity over the years was level of education. Don't worry if you don't have a doctoral degree; most experts think it's not the years of formal education per se that benefit memory but rather the habit of being inquisitive and engaged in learning new things. A high level of education might help in this regard by establishing a habit of reading regularly and doing other things to challenge yourself intellectually.

We believe that intellectual enrichment and learning promote physiological and structural changes in the brain, ultimately leading to increased synaptic density and neuronal interconnection. Remember that neuronal connections are critical for the formation of memories. So the "educated brain" may possess more of these pathways and, therefore, a larger anatomical infrastructure to support learning and memory.

A well-educated brain can more effectively withstand age-related neuronal loss than a poorly educated brain. This added resiliency forms the basis for the concept of cognitive reserve, which is used to explain the finding that people with high baseline intelligence are less likely to be diagnosed with dementia than people with lower baseline intelligence.

When patients ask what sorts of things they can do to maintain mental activity, I advise them to identify ideas and issues that pique their curiosity, that engage and excite them, that challenge them to learn. Travel, theater, community service, a book group, a new hobby or sport, adult education, designing a new house, French cooking, learning a musical instrument, local politics, karate—whatever it is for you.

Smoking

If a smoker and a nonsmoker were each to take a memory test, the nonsmoker would probably do better. We've known for years that smokers don't remember names and faces as well as nonsmokers do. But we didn't know the extent of the disparity until recently, when a large study found that smokers exhibited a far steeper decline in memory and related cognitive functions than did nonsmokers.

In a 2004 study published in the journal *Neurology*, 9,209 people ages sixty-five and older were evaluated on an annual basis with the Mini-Mental State Examination, a standard test of cognitive functions, for several years. Scores declined slightly for most participants during this period, but the decline was five times greater for smokers than for people who never smoked. The decline was most pronounced among people who smoked the most cigarettes over the longest period of time.

A link between cigarette smoking and memory has also been reported in research with middle-aged individuals. A 2003 British study found a direct connection between smoking and weaker verbal memory performance in people between the ages of forty-three and fifty-three.

There are several ways that smoking might impair cognitive function, primarily related to its role as a major risk factor for cerebrovascular disease. Smoking damages the lungs, and good lung function is important for optimal memory function in aging. Smoking also constricts blood vessels, thereby depriving the brain of the oxygen necessary to nourish and support neurons. Nutritional factors may also play a role in the smoking-memory connection; smokers tend to have lower intake of antioxidants and higher levels of cholesterol and triglycerides. There are many unknowns, but one bit of encouraging news is that smoking cessation seems to benefit the brain. In the previously cited 2004 study, former smokers exhibited less cognitive decline than current smokers.

Illicit Drug Use

Marijuana, ecstasy, and other illegal drugs can impair memory and related brain functions. The effects are not only evident while the drugs are being used but can persist for weeks and months afterward.

The active substance in marijuana, Delta (9)-tetrahydrocannabinol, engenders psychoactive effects by attaching to receptors in the brain for cannabinoid. Cannabinoid receptors are plentiful in the hippocampus, amygdala, and cerebral cortex, regions that are crucial for forming memories. People who smoke marijuana heavily and over a long period of time score lower than nonusers on tests of attention, short-term memory, and learning. In a study published in *Neurology* in 2002, these impairments lasted nearly a month after the marijuana users abstained from the drug. We don't know the degree to which marijuana-related memory problems are reversible with abstinence.

Regular users of ecstasy, or 3,4-methylenedioxymethamphetamine (MDMA), have trouble forming and recalling long-term memories. In a survey of 763 people published in the *Journal of Psychopharmacology* in 2004, ecstasy users were 23 percent more likely than nonusers to report difficulty with long-term memory. It stands to reason that ecstasy would impair memory because it reduces levels of serotonin and dopamine, neurotransmitters that are important for memory.

People who use cocaine have difficulty with various aspects of memory. In a study conducted at UCLA, cocaine abusers scored lower than nonusers on tests of working memory and long-term recall. Another study found that problems with verbal memory in cocaine users persisted even after cessation of use for forty-five days.

We don't know how long the harmful effects of various illicit drugs linger in the brain. But quitting certainly can't do harm and may restore some or all of the memory function that was lost.

Toxic Exposure

Memory loss and difficulty concentrating are among the most common effects of exposure to toxic chemicals—including lead, mercury, petroleum, and various chemical solvents—at home and in the workplace. Lead poisoning can result from inhaling lead dust from deteriorating paint in an old home or from drinking contaminated tap water. Some paints, dyes, and inks used in artwork contain mercury and solvents that are neurotoxic and can impair memory. Neurotoxic substances are also present in pesticides used in farming and home gardening; darkroom chemicals; and chemicals used in metalwork and woodwork.

Aluminum and Alzheimer's Disease

You might have heard that exposure to aluminum can cause Alzheimer's disease. Scientists have been studying this issue for many years, ever since finding that aluminum accumulates in the abnormal brain tissue of people with Alzheimer's disease. The evidence has been difficult to sort out, and many studies have offered contradictory findings.

You can be exposed to aluminum in drinking water, in foods cooked in aluminum pots and pans, and possibly in foods and beverages packaged in aluminum. Some antiperspirants contain aluminum, which can be absorbed through the skin. But such environmental exposures tend to be extremely small. Although scientists continue to study the Alzheimer's-aluminum connection, most experts discount aluminum as a significant risk factor for the disease.

You can reduce your exposure to toxic chemicals by taking these precautions:

- **Lead house paint.** If you live in a house built in 1978 or earlier, it may contain lead paint. It's unnecessary to remove the paint if it's in good condition. If it's not, don't attempt to remove it yourself, as this can release harmful lead dust into the air. Contact the U.S. Department of Housing and Urban Development for information on finding an approved contractor to do the work.
- **Drinking water.** If your water comes from a public water system, obtain a copy of the system's annual water quality report to see if the levels of any toxic chemicals exceed government standards. Keep in mind, however, that when toxic chemicals are present in drinking water, the source is often the pipes in individual homes. You can measure the amount of lead and other chemicals in your tap water by using one of the U.S. Environmental Protection

Agency–approved water-testing kits available in hardware stores and elsewhere. There are also several water filters on the market that can remove lead and other toxic chemicals.

- **Art supplies and household chemicals.** When using paints and other art materials, make sure you work in a well-ventilated area. Follow the safe use directions on the label of pesticides, solvents, and any other chemicals you use. Wear a protective mask.
- **Carbon monoxide.** Prevent carbon monoxide exposure by getting a regular inspection of your home heating system and your automobile's exhaust system.

Self-Help or Professional Help?

It's no coincidence that this is one of the longest chapters in the book—there are many causes of memory loss. You can detect and remedy some of them on your own by following my recommendations—challenging your mind, eating a healthier diet, and getting more physical activity—as well as the program I outline in Chapters 9 and 10. But many causes of memory problems are themselves illnesses (or treatments of illnesses) that require medical attention. In the next chapter, I discuss when to see your doctor.

CHAPTER 6

When to See a Doctor

In July 2002 David, an extraordinarily successful fifty-five-year-old entertainment executive, traveled from Los Angeles to my office in Boston for a consultation. David was an imposing figure, a large man with a somewhat pressured manner who was clearly used to moving through his world in full command of all that transpired around him. He was engaging and exhibited a wry sense of humor, which only partially obscured his anxiety as he began to tell me his story.

David's Memory Problems

David worried that he was "losing it." The *it* referred to his ability to absorb, integrate, and analyze the hundreds of bits of information that arrived at his desk daily via phone calls, e-mails, faxes, and so on. He told me that he used to have a "photographic" memory but that he now experienced his memory as a "faded watercolor," in which previously sharp details had become indiscernible. To illustrate the problem, he described a recent morning walk through the studio of a television show that his division was producing. As usual, he made mental notes of ten issues that required his personal attention. But fifteen minutes later, when he was back in his office, he could recall only half of the items on his list.

I asked if any of his associates or family members had commented on problems with his memory or performance. He said they had not.

When asked about other changes that he was concerned about, he mentioned feeling more short-tempered and impatient. He recounted an episode in which he yelled at his eleven-year-old daughter, who had accidentally knocked over a glass of milk at the dinner table. Other changes included a weight gain of ten pounds over the past six months (due, in part, to a donut-based breakfast) and difficulty sleeping. He hardly exercised anymore, and he was spending more and more time in the office.

When I asked about alcohol use, he hesitatingly acknowledged that alcohol had become a "mini issue." He had been drinking at business lunches and had upped his evening drink to "two or three." I then asked about his mood and probed his attitude toward his life, and he confided that the things he used to enjoy most in life, such as opera, photography, and tennis, had "lost some of their luster."

David's Medical History

In taking his medical history, I learned that David had hypertension and high cholesterol. Though he was taking medication for both conditions, they weren't being adequately controlled. He had been to a hospital emergency department five months earlier with chest pain, which turned out to be benign. A recent physical examination, blood tests, and a chest x-ray were normal. His primary care physician had also ordered a brain MRI, which was normal.

David had a family history of cardiovascular disease; his father succumbed to a stroke at age sixty-six, and his mother had severe heart disease and had suffered multiple heart attacks. An older brother had recently undergone four-vessel cardiac bypass surgery. When I asked about any familial history of neurological problems, David recalled that his grandmother had become "senile" and was ultimately unable to remember names of family members or take care of herself. He then spontaneously commented, "You know, it did occur to me that maybe I'm getting what she had."

Memory Myth: My Mother Had Alzheimer's, So I'm Bound to Get It, Too

Having a first- or second-degree relative (sibling, parent, aunt, uncle, grandparent) with Alzheimer's disease does not mean that you're destined to get it. Only the rarest form of Alzheimer's disease, the early-onset familial type, is unequivocally genetically transmitted. But even if your mother or another close relative had early-onset Alzheimer's disease, unless you carry one of the genetic mutations that cause it, your risk is no higher than that of someone without a family history of the disease.

David's Examination

Tests of cognitive function showed that David was having mild difficulty with tasks calling for sustained attention and concentration. Although this difficulty limited how much information he was able to take in at one time, his ability to remember information that he had effectively learned was normal. In fact, his performance on many of the cognitive tests was in the superior range.

My impression was that David's problem with everyday memory was being driven by a number of factors and that they could be addressed and reversed. When we met for a follow-up consultation, I reassured him that I did not believe he was following in his grandmother's footsteps. He responded with the same visible relief that all patients convey when their worst fears are disproved. His response opened the door for the ensuing discussion of the changes he needed to make in order to reclaim the edge he felt he had begun to lose.

David's Memory Treatment Plan

I encouraged David to commit himself to a lifestyle that emphasized brain fitness. We discussed his risk factors for cerebrovascular disease and what he needed to do in order to reduce them. These included maintaining a heart-healthy diet and adopting a vigilant stance with his blood pressure and cholesterol. To get started, I referred him to a clinical nutritionist who works with our team, and I suggested that he get a copy of Dr. Walter Willett's excellent book *Eat, Drink, and Be Healthy* (2001). I encouraged him to begin monitoring his blood pressure with a device he could buy at a pharmacy.

We then reviewed the effect of excessive and continuous stress on cardiovascular health, emotional well-being, and brain function. I pointed out that he had relinquished many of the activities that used to provide him with opportunities for recreation and stress release. He understood how time *away* from his work could paradoxically result in greater professional productivity. He promised to resume his workout routine and get back on schedule for weekly tennis matches with his oldest son. Without needing a lecture from me, he indicated his intention to reduce his alcohol consumption by regaining his discipline during his business lunches.

We also discussed practical cognitive strategies—for example, making written notes or using a PDA to record information on the spot for future reference.

I suspected that if David took all of these steps, his memory, as well as his sleep and mood, would improve. If not, we could explore further to see if he had an underlying sleep disorder and if his moodiness was due to depression.

We agreed that he could call me if needed but that we would meet again in six months to take stock of his progress.

Six Months Later: A Sharper Memory

It was winter in Boston with a foot of snow on the ground when David visited next. He looked tan and relaxed (living in Southern California would account for the tan), and he had slimmed down noticeably. We spent a moment talking about the new show he was working on, and it was clear that he was enjoying his work in a way that he had not when I initially met him.

David had done very well in following the recommendations we had developed, and they were making a difference. He had resumed tennis matches with his son, and though he had lost "eighteen times in a row," he looked forward more than ever to the chance that the matches gave him to "just hang out and catch up." His blood pressure had dropped so much that he was hopeful that he would soon be able to shed one of the antihypertensive medicines he was taking. His cholesterol level had dropped below 200, and he was committed to further improvement. He had begun using a handheld microcassette recorder to make note of observations and thoughts that required future attention.

When we spoke about his memory concerns, he related that since our visit, he had had the opportunity to compare himself with many of his peers and learned that, if anything, he was doing better than they were. I administered a follow-up battery of cognitive tests and found significant improvement in the areas that had previously been mildly abnormal.

In many ways, David was an ideal patient. He was insightful, intelligent, and motivated. He took my advice seriously and had a positive outcome. Above all, he was proactive—he was concerned about his memory and he sought help.

Do You Need a Memory Evaluation?

If you're concerned enough about your memory to wonder if something's wrong, you should see your doctor. Begin with a consultation with your primary care physician. Because this doctor knows you and your medical history, he or she is in an advantageous position to assess the big picture of your health and consider the more common medical and psychological conditions that can cause memory loss.

Don't expect to walk out of your primary care physician's office with a diagnosis. There's no single test that can pinpoint the cause of memory loss. A more typical experience is for your doctor to do some preliminary detective work: ask you questions about your symptoms, give you a thorough physical examination, review your medications, and run tests for medical conditions that can cause or contribute to memory loss. There is considerable variability among primary care physicians with regard to expertise, interest, and time availability for pursuing a comprehensive evaluation for a memory concern. Not all primary care doctors feel comfortable or prepared to evaluate cognitive problems in detail.

If your doctor tells you, "You don't have Alzheimer's disease, so don't worry—it's just normal aging," but you are still concerned about your memory, don't be shy about saying so. Some primary care physicians tend to be dismissive of subtle memory complaints in an otherwise well-functioning person. Some have too few categories to rely on in making sense of a memory issue (that is, either the patient has Alzheimer's disease or nothing is wrong). Although Alzheimer's disease accounts for the vast majority of degenerative dementias in older people, many other diseases and conditions can cause dementia, as discussed in Chapter 5. By the same token, although memory dysfunction is the single most common cognitive complaint, brain disorders can produce many other cognitive symptoms.

Some primary care doctors may not ask the questions that would lead to identification of less obvious causes of memory loss, such as depression or a sleep disorder. To be fair, there are many primary care physicians who do take the time and have the knowledge base to obtain a good initial workup. Others recognize their limitations in this area and will refer to a specialist right away.

For the record, most people who seek a memory evaluation for themselves have a treatable condition that's causing their problems. People ultimately diagnosed with Alzheimer's disease usually come to the doctor's office because of concerns raised by family members or another physician.

When You Visit Your Doctor

Your doctor will need to review your medical history, perform a physical examination, and run some tests to determine whether your memory difficulties are benign in nature or are due to an underlying medical condition.

Questions to Discuss with Your Doctor

Your doctor will probably begin by asking you about recent memory problems to define the parameters of your symptoms. Here are some typical questions:

- How long have you been having trouble with your memory?
- Did the trouble come on gradually or suddenly?
- Has the problem been getting better or getting worse, or has it remained about the same?
- What sorts of things have become more difficult to remember?
- Is the problem interfering with your usual activities, such as reading, cooking, or performing on the job?
- Have other people—friends, family members, or colleagues—independently commented on your memory problem?
- Are you taking any medications?
- Do you have any current health problems?
- What medical problems have you had in the past?
- Do you have a family history of illnesses that can affect brain function and memory, such as high blood pressure, high cholesterol, heart disease, Alzheimer's disease, or other neurological disorders?
- Have you been feeling depressed or stressed?

Answers to these questions can indicate whether your symptoms are typical of a memory disorder, such as Alzheimer's disease or mild cognitive impairment, an age-related condition that is less severe than Alzheimer's disease but may be a precursor to it. Symptoms that distinguish age-related memory loss from mild cognitive impairment and Alzheimer's disease are listed in Table 6.1.

Memory problems related to Alzheimer's disease usually commence insidiously and progress relentlessly; an abrupt decline in memory usually suggests other causes, such as a more acute neurological problem or perhaps a medication you've recently started.

TABLE 6.1 Symptoms of Age-Related Memory Loss, Mild Cognitive Impairment, and Alzheimer's Disease

Symptoms	Normal Age-Related Memory Loss	Mild Cognitive Impairment (Amnesic Type)	Dementia
Difficulty remembering names, appointments, and other everyday information	Occasional	More frequent	Most of the time
Problems with memory and concentration that can be measured by standardized tests	None; test performance is in line with age peers	Mild to moderate impairment compared to age peers	Moderate to severe impairment compared to age peers
Problems with cognitive functions other than memory (e.g., making and executing plans, solving problems, making judgments)	Rare; problems are subtle when present and do not have an impact on everyday function	Rare to mild deficits with occasional slight impact on daily activity	Moderate to severe impairment with clear impact on everyday function and activities
Difficulty with activities of daily living (e.g., dressing, brushing teeth)	None	None	Moderate to severe problems in aspects of self-care
Increased difficulty with household tasks and hobbies	None	Occasional difficulty with complex activities	Moderate to severe impairment

Your doctor will need to know whether you're taking any medications that might affect your memory. If so, and if you started taking it shortly before you noticed a change in your memory, then the diagnostic process might focus on that drug. Depending on the medication, your doctor might ask you to stop taking it for a while or prescribe an alternative drug to see whether your memory improves.

But even if a medication is a possible culprit, your doctor should also give you a thorough examination to determine if there are other medical or psychological factors that might be contributing to your memory problem.

The Physical Examination

Because a multitude of physical and psychological conditions can affect your memory, your physician will review your personal medical history. And because many relevant medical factors and disorders are heritable or tend to run in families, your checkup will include questions about your family medical history.

As part of your physical examination, your doctor will probably:

- Measure your vital signs (by taking your temperature, blood pressure, and pulse)
- Examine your head, neck, eyes, ears, nose, and throat
- Palpate the lymph nodes in your neck
- Listen to your heart and lungs
- Screen your blood for signs of thyroid dysfunction, kidney disease, diabetes, anemia, infection, cancer, vitamin deficiency, and elevated cholesterol
- Analyze your urine for signs of kidney and thyroid problems
- Obtain a chest x-ray to check for lung disease
- Perform a basic neurological evaluation, including testing your cranial nerves, reflexes, coordination, gait, and sensorimotor function
- Perform a digital prostate examination (men)
- Perform a breast examination (women)

Your primary care doctor should also assess your psychological health. He or she might ask whether you have been under a lot of stress lately or whether you've been feeling down. If your doctor doesn't ask you about these issues and they apply to you, you should say so; stress and depression are *treatable* causes of memory dysfunction.

Depending on what your doctor learns from the examination and from talking to you about your symptoms, he or she might recommend additional tests or refer you to a specialist for a consultation.

Neuropsychological Testing

When you think of memory testing, chances are that you are thinking of the kinds of evaluations that constitute neuropsychological testing. Neuropsychological testing comprises a battery of tests of mental abilities that comprehensively evaluates overall cognitive function. Neuropsychologists are psychologists with specialized training in brain behavior relationships and brain disorders. Some neuropsychologists utilize technicians to assist in test administration.

A neuropsychological examination begins with a careful review of your concerns and medical history. The testing process typically relies on a combination of oral questioning, paper-and-pencil tests, and computer-based assessment. Although assessment of memory function is a major focus, the evaluation also explores aspects of attention, language, visuospatial processing, reasoning, problem solving, and overall modulation of thinking and responding. The assessment battery might include additional tests or questionnaires to gauge your mood or survey symptoms in other areas. Not all neuropsychologists use the same tests, but they all examine the same spectrum of cognitive functions. Some neuropsychologists practice independently, and others are based in hospitals and medical centers.

The purpose of these tests is to determine if your memory and other cognitive abilities fall within normal limits or if the findings suggest a disorder such as depression, mild cognitive impairment, or Alzheimer's disease. But what's normal for you isn't necessarily normal for another person. The neuropsychologist will interpret and analyze the test results within the context of several important variables that influence memory and cognitive ability, such as your age, your estimated baseline intelligence, and your level of education. The distinction between normal and abnormal test performance may be different for a person with a high IQ and an extensive education than for a person with a lower IQ and fewer years of education.

Research at Harvard Medical School published in 2004 looked specifically at the effect of IQ on the interpretation of memory test results in a group of highly intelligent elderly individuals. Instead of using general normative data, the researchers found that using cutoff scores adjusted for IQ more accurately predicted future diagnosis of mild cognitive impairment and Alzheimer's disease. This finding suggests that what's "normal" for someone of low or average IQ is actually below normal for someone with a high IQ. But there is some controversy among neuropsychologists regarding the use of IQ in the interpretation of test scores. The assumption that intelligence correlates closely with other aspects of cognitive function, such as memory, is not universally accepted.

Here are the cognitive domains that are assessed in a neuropsychological evaluation:

- **Attention.** There are many tests that can be used to assess attentional function. For example, the Digit Span test involves listening to and then repeating increasingly long series of numbers. Tests of sustained attention entail maintaining vigilance over a more extended period of time. One test involves viewing a computer screen that flashes a random series of letters with the instruction to respond to a target stimulus—for example, the letter *A*—by pressing a computer key. In a more challenging version, the instruction is to respond to the letter *A* only when it follows the letter *Y*.

- **Memory.** The most common type of memory test involves listening to or reading information and recalling it immediately afterward and then recalling it again ten to thirty minutes later. The information may consist of a list of words or a brief narrative story. Other memory tests use visual information; you study a picture or a design and then reproduce it from memory. The neuropsychologist might also examine your long-term memory by asking you

Memory Testing on the Internet

If you search "memory tests" or "Alzheimer's screening test" on the Internet, you'll find a number of websites featuring self-administered "tests" of memory function. You might wonder if these tests are valid and if they are worth doing.

My response is, that depends.

The better sites are information based and provide structured questionnaires that review the most prominent symptoms of memory disorders. They do not purport to make an "e-diagnosis" but rather encourage the user to seek appropriate evaluation and care if indicated. Many of these types of sites are sponsored by memory clinics associated with university medical centers and can be thought of as offering a public health service, much in the same way as the National Institutes of Health provides information about diseases free of charge to the public.

Other sites are sponsored by pharmaceutical companies with the ultimate goal of steering customers toward prescription medications. Pharmaceutical companies have become increasingly interested in direct marketing to consumers. Although raising consciousness through information is a good thing, it is wise to

questions about your personal history or factual information you may have learned in the past.

- **Executive functions.** Executive functions are high-level cognitive operations that include reasoning, problem solving, and planning. Executive functions refer to the overall management of thinking and behavior and include the capability to initiate a behavioral response, to inhibit inappropriate or incorrect responses, and to flexibly shift responses depending on circumstances. Along with memory and naming, executive functions are among the first areas of thinking to become impaired in people with Alzheimer's disease.

consider the source and its motivations when evaluating the information.

Still other memory testing websites are sponsored by medical care companies. Along with blood sugar self-testing in diabetes, pregnancy testing kits, and low-cost blood pressure monitors, their approach fits within the general framework of home-based medical testing. These sites typically charge a user fee for accessing an online screening test or responding to an interactive questionnaire. The user is provided with feedback on test performance or risk for having a memory disorder. Some of these sites offer subscription services, which enable you to retest yourself over a period of time. But the fact is that the tests used by these sites have not been scientifically validated.

Claims that a problem as complex as memory dysfunction can be diagnosed by "remote control" are irresponsible. There's no harm in taking memory tests on the Internet for fun, the same way you might try a puzzle in a magazine. However, if you are concerned about yourself or a family member, seek professional evaluation.

One test of executive function is the Trail-Making test. On the first part of this test, you'll see a page with circles, each with a number inside. You'll have to connect the circles in numerical order as quickly as possible—a relatively simple task. On the second part of the test, you'll see circles containing either a number or a letter. This time, you'll have to connect the circles by alternating between numbers and letters: 1 to A to 2 to B to 3 to C and so on. Both speed and accuracy are scored.

- **Language.** Subtle problems with naming and word finding can be early symptoms of Alzheimer's disease or a rare neurological disorder known as primary progressive aphasia, in which language function is gradually impaired. You will be asked to name common objects or pictured items. You might also be asked to follow instructions as a way of testing language comprehension and praxis, the ability to carry out a behavioral response to a verbal instruction. Other tests of language ability include comprehension of written material, repetition of phonemically complex words and phrases, and narrative writing in response to a standard stimulus picture.

- **Spatial ability.** Spatial ability involves analyzing visual information, such as shapes, faces, and routes between locations on a map. Tests include drawing and copying designs, solving maze puzzles, and using blocks to construct a specific pattern. The right hemisphere of the brain has a special role in spatial tasks like these, so difficulty with these tests may indicate a problem affecting this brain region. In some cases, symptoms that suggest a dysfunction of the right side of the brain are early symptoms of the so-called visual variant of Alzheimer's disease. Before you jump to the conclusion that your difficulty reading a map reflects a neurological disorder, be assured that all people have a profile of cognitive strengths and weaknesses; relative difficulty in one area may reflect nothing more than a normal developmental pattern.

Specialized Tests

If your medical examination and test results suggest the possibility of a brain disorder, your doctor will probably refer you for one or more specialized tests. The following tests are used in the evaluation and diagnosis of a wide range of neurological conditions.

Lumbar Puncture

This test, also called a spinal tap, involves drawing a small sample of the cerebrospinal fluid that surrounds your brain and spinal cord. The fluid sample is removed from between two vertebrae in your lower back as you lie on your side. The fluid is then analyzed in order to determine whether there is evidence of infection or inflammation of the central nervous system (brain and spinal cord).

Electroencephalogram (EEG)

An EEG measures brain waves, or electrical activity in the brain. Electrodes placed on your scalp and possibly your face pick up brain waves and convert them to a visual signal, which can be displayed on a machine called an electroencephalograph. Older electroencephalography machines traced these visual signals on continuously moving paper; computers are now used to record, display, and assist in analyzing EEG data. An abnormal pattern of brain waves can help identify epilepsy, sleep disorders, neurotoxic states, and other brain disorders.

Structural Brain Imaging

Several diagnostic tests produce structural images of the brain. Magnetic resonance imaging (MRI), a high-resolution structural imaging technique, can show the shape, size, and contour of the brain. Each new generation of MRI scanners is more sensitive than the one before, and the newest ones can produce spectacular high-resolution images of the brain. Although brain atrophy can be quite subtle in the earliest stages of Alzheimer's disease, high-quality imaging can often reveal tissue loss in key brain structures, including the hippocampus.

Computed tomography (CT) scanning also yields a structural image of the brain. CT utilizes a rotating x-ray device coupled to a computer, which reassembles the data into a cross-sectional image. The image can be modeled three-dimensionally.

Both MRI and CT can identify structural abnormalities within the brain that are characteristic of many conditions that cause memory problems, including hydrocephalus (an excess of cerebrospinal fluid beneath the skull), subdural hematoma (blood pooling beneath the skull), or a brain tumor. All of these conditions increase pressure inside the brain, leading to memory impairment and other cognitive and neurological symptoms. These conditions are often treatable, particularly if detected early.

Brain imaging is also used to diagnose stroke, which can impair memory and other brain functions.

Functional Brain Imaging

If your structural imaging is normal but your doctor suspects that you might have Alzheimer's disease or another type of degenerative condition, he or she might also recommend a single photon emission computed tomography (SPECT) scan or a positron emission tomography (PET) scan. Rather than producing a picture of brain structure, these imaging techniques look at how the brain is functioning. SPECT traces perfusion (blood flow), and PET maps glucose metabolism. Decreased perfusion or energy metabolism in the temporal and parietal regions of the brain is the functional "signature" of Alzheimer's disease. Other brain disorders produce distinctive functional imaging patterns. These scans can reveal abnormalities even when an MRI appears normal.

Functional MRI (fMRI) is a newer imaging methodology that is being used extensively in research to determine which brain regions are activated during different types of cognitive processing. It uses conventional MRI technology, but it acquires a series of images so rapidly that they can be analyzed to reveal subtle changes in blood flow during performance of a specific cognitive task. In all likelihood, fMRI will soon gain acceptance as another useful diagnostic clinical tool.

Cerebral Angiogram

A cerebral angiogram is obtained when there is a need to evaluate the blood vessels that perfuse the brain. A long thin tube (catheter) is placed into an artery in the groin and advanced through the body until it reaches the carotid artery in the neck. An instrument called a fluoroscope provides a moving image of the catheter as it is being inserted, allowing the doctor to carefully guide it to a precise location. A contrast dye is injected through the catheter, and x-ray images are produced. The contrast dye causes the blood vessels to be clearly visualized so that blockages or abnormal vascular anatomy can be identified.

Genetic Testing

Blood tests are available that can determine if you carry one of the genetic mutations or variants associated with Alzheimer's disease or one of the other extremely rare genetically transmitted degenerative disorders. In people with a family history of *early-onset familial Alzheimer's disease*, a rare form of Alzheimer's that can appear as early as the fourth decade of life, genetic testing will identify mutations in three genes: presenilin 1, presenilin 2, and the amyloid precursor protein gene. Mutations in these genes are associated with early-onset familial Alzheimer's, which accounts for about 5 percent of all cases of the disease.

In contrast, the vast majority of Alzheimer's disease is designated *sporadic*, meaning that there is no known cause. However, variants of one gene—ApoE—influence your risk of developing the disease at some point during your lifetime. The ApoE gene has three alleles, or forms: e2, e3, and e4. Because you inherit one allele from each parent, there are six possible allele combinations: e2/e2, e2/e3, e2/e4, e3/e3, e3/e4, and e4/e4. The e4 allele is associated with the greatest probability of developing Alzheimer's disease; having two e4 alleles places you in the highest risk group. On the other hand, possessing two e2 alleles places you in a reduced risk category.

Between 35 and 50 percent of people with Alzheimer's disease have at least one copy of the ApoE e4 allele. That said, inheriting a copy of the e4 allele doesn't mean that you will definitely get Alzheimer's disease, and not inheriting the allele doesn't mean that you won't, so this genetic information may not be highly meaningful for most people. However, for people who are currently exhibiting symptoms of a dementia, ApoE testing can lend weight for or against Alzheimer's disease as the underlying cause.

I want to emphasize that even if you do have a family history of early-onset familial Alzheimer's, that doesn't mean that you will absolutely develop the disorder yourself or that you should have a genetic test. Even if you knew that you had one of the disease-producing mutations, we do not yet possess the therapy to change your odds of manifesting the disorder. If you don't want

Genetic Testing for Memory Impairment

Many of my patients think that having a genetic test for Alzheimer's disease will tell them whether they will get the disorder. But it won't—at least not for most people. People with a family history of early-onset familial Alzheimer's disease can learn if they carry one of the genetic markers that convey a 100 percent probability of developing the disease. Inheriting a specific mutation in one of three genes—presenilin 1, presenilin 2, and the amyloid precursor protein gene—means that you will get the disease; not having a mutation means that, despite your family history, your risk is no greater than for a person without the mutation.

There are many ethical and psychological issues to consider before having a genetic test. For patients with a positive family history of early-onset disease, the outcome of the genetic test is definitive. Although they may want to know their genotype for any number of reasons, a positive test is almost always emotionally devastating. If a patient insists on knowing his or her genetic destiny, I make certain that the person consults with a genetic

to know your genetic profile, you shouldn't be tested. If you decide to be tested, make sure that you receive counseling both before and afterward so that you understand exactly what the results mean and have the emotional and psychological support you need to cope with them. See the sidebar "Genetic Testing for Memory Impairment" for more information.

Other Specialty Consultations

Because memory loss can have such a wide array of causes, the diagnostic process may require input from additional medical specialists. Your primary care physician might refer you to one or more of the following types of doctors to follow up on particular findings from your initial checkup:

counselor before and after being tested in order to be in the best position to make an informed decision and to have the emotional support to cope with the results.

Some patients without a family history of early-onset Alzheimer's disease express a desire to have the ApoE test, which indicates the risk of developing the most common form of Alzheimer's disease but doesn't offer definitive information. I ask them: How would knowing this information affect your view of yourself and your life? Can you handle the information? I'm also concerned about the possibility that some people might be denied employment, health insurance, or access to other resources if they test positive for an e4 allele, the variant of ApoE that conveys increased risk.

The genetics of Alzheimer's disease and other memory disorders are a work in progress. Once we have true preventive treatment in our therapeutic arsenal, unraveling the genetic secrets of this disease will be even more critical.

- **Neurologist.** A neurologist can diagnose and treat a wide range of central nervous system conditions that cause memory and cognitive symptoms. Many neurologists subspecialize in specific disorders, such as Parkinson's disease, epilepsy, or dementia.
- **Psychiatrist.** If there is a question of depression or anxiety, a psychiatrist can make a definitive diagnosis and recommend a course of treatment.
- **Neurosurgeon.** If medical testing indicates a structural abnormality in the brain, such as a tumor, vascular malformation, or hydrocephalus that requires surgery, you will need to see a neurosurgeon.
- **Endocrinologist.** An endocrinologist might be needed to evaluate and treat hormonal problems, such as a thyroid disorder, that might be affecting your memory.

Normal Aging or Dementia: A Questionnaire

How do you know when memory loss is an early symptom of Alzheimer's disease or another type of dementia? There's no question that severe, progressive memory loss is a hallmark of dementia, but recent research suggests that forgetfulness alone is not a perfect predictor of Alzheimer's disease. In an article published in the *Archives of Neurology* in 2000, researchers at Harvard Medical School found that responses to eight standard clinical questions predicted with a high degree of accuracy whether people with memory impairment would remain stable, decline, or improve. The eight questions were derived from three categories—judgment and problem solving, home and hobbies, and personal care—as follows:

Judgment and Problem Solving

1. Do you have increased difficulty handling problems (for example, are you relying more on others to help solve problems or make plans)?
2. Is there a change in your pattern of driving that is not the result of vision problems (for example, a greater degree of caution, trouble in making decisions, and so on)?
3. Is your judgment less sound than it used to be?
4. Are you having increased difficulty managing finances (for example, maintaining a checkbook, paying bills, making complex financial decisions)?

- **Cardiologist.** You will be referred to a cardiologist if your medical evaluation suggests that you have heart disease.

After the Testing

Diagnosing the cause of memory impairment is no simple matter. It takes time and often requires visiting several doctors and undergoing a number of tests. In many cases, neuropsychological eval-

5. Are you having more difficulty handling emergencies? Have you been making unsafe decisions? Do you rely more on cues from other people in order to react appropriately?

Home and Hobbies

6. Are you having increased difficulty performing household tasks, such as cooking or learning how to use new appliances?

7. Has there been any change in your ability to pursue your hobbies? For example, do you spend less time on complex hobbies? Do you have more trouble following the rules of games? Do you read less, or do you need to reread more often in order to understand what you've read?

Personal Care

8. Do you need prompting to shave or shower?

Scoring: People in the study who answered yes to *all* of these questions were most likely to develop Alzheimer's disease within three years.

The purpose of this quiz (and the others in this book) is to indicate if you have symptoms that warrant further evaluation. It is not intended to diagnose a memory disorder. If you answered yes to four or more of the questions, see your physician.

uation must be repeated at intervals over time in order to arrive at a definitive understanding of the problem. What happens after that depends on the diagnosis. In the next chapter, I discuss how doctors recognize the difference between normal memory lapses and memory disorders.

CHAPTER 7

Memory Disorders

One morning in June 2002, a young man named Steven arrived at my office for an evaluation, having been referred by his primary care physician. Steven was pleasant and amiable, and he easily made conversation. Although he had difficulty providing detail about his history, he was able to tell me that he had been having memory problems since being injured in a motor vehicle accident six months earlier. He spoke somewhat vaguely about his current circumstances: where he was living, family members in the area, and so on. Although he could recall very little about the specifics of his work, he was able to provide a step-by-step depiction of the process for handcrafting a leather vest, which had been his profession until the time of the injury.

I began the examination, administering a series of subtests from the Wechsler Intelligence Scale to gauge Steven's overall intellectual ability. He performed extremely well, and I estimated his IQ to lie in the superior range. After about an hour of testing, Steven needed to use the men's room. I showed him the way, pointing to a lavatory that was twenty steps down the hall from my office.

I was waiting in the hall halfway between the restroom and my office when he emerged less than two minutes later. He looked both ways and began walking uncertainly in my direction. He made direct eye contact with me as he passed by and nodded, flashing a warm smile. I caught up with him a moment later and asked if we had ever met. Steven shuffled his feet and looked away, remarking that he did not think so.

Steven was amnesic. He had sustained an anoxic injury (disruption of oxygen flow to the brain) during the motor vehicle accident. Despite spending well over an hour in face-to-face interaction with me, a brief interruption was sufficient to erase any memory of me or what he had been doing two minutes earlier. He later explained that he had developed a habit of pleasantly acknowledging people he encountered on the assumption that he may have met them before, although he was utterly incapable of recalling the specifics.

When we speak of memory disorders, we mean neuropsychological disorders in which the cardinal symptom is memory dysfunction. These conditions are distinct from the wide range of illnesses discussed in Chapter 5, such as depression or heart disease, that can secondarily cause memory loss as one of many symptoms. Primary memory disorders include amnesia, mild cognitive impairment, and dementia; this chapter will provide an overview of them.

Normal Versus Abnormal Forgetting

Tests of memory and related cognitive functions can help distinguish memory disorders from normal, age-related memory loss. And make no mistake: age-related memory loss is *not* a disorder. However, two memory disorders—mild cognitive impairment and dementia—do become more common with age, leading memory researchers to wonder if there is any relationship between them and age-related memory loss.

Experts disagree about the answer. Some say that mild cognitive impairment and dementia are entirely distinct from age-related memory loss. We refer to this view as the discontinuity model. In this view, age-related memory loss is an effect of the normal developmental evolution of the brain in the same way as diminished bone density is the normal and inevitable destiny of the aging human skeleton. On the other hand, discontinuity adherents view dementia as the product of a pathophysiological disease process, a divergence from normal health and development.

Other experts view age-related memory loss, mild cognitive impairment, and dementia as points on a single continuum extending from normal to abnormal memory. This is not to say that age-related memory loss will inevitably lead to mild cognitive impairment and then to dementia. How far an individual progresses along this continuum depends on a number of factors, many of which have been reviewed in earlier chapters. However, supporters of the "continuity hypothesis" believe that the pathophysiological process that underlies age-related memory compromise is essentially the same across all points. The implication of this view is that each and every one of us would ultimately arrive at a state of dementia if we lived long enough.

We won't know which model is more accurate until we learn more precisely what happens in the brain with age-related memory loss, mild cognitive impairment, and dementia. But we do know that there are several ways to reduce or reverse age-related memory problems, whereas at this point we do not have actual disease-modifying therapy for mild cognitive impairment or dementia.

Amnesia

Amnesia is a profound defect in the ability to form new memories, to remember existing memories, or to do both. The inability to create new memories is called *anterograde amnesia*, and the inability to recall old memories is called *retrograde amnesia*.

There are many misconceptions about amnesia. For one thing, unlike the other memory disorders, amnesia does not rob people of their general intellectual ability. In addition, it is not a single condition; rather, there are a number of subtypes of amnesia, each with different features and different causes.

Perhaps the most pervasive misconception about amnesia is that it affects all kinds of memory. In fact, it is mainly new learn-

Core Features of Amnesia

Impaired recall of episodic memories

Rapid forgetting with impaired ability to form new declarative memories

Unimpaired overall intelligence

Normal attention and working memory capacity

Relatively preserved skill learning and procedural memory

ing and the episodic form of declarative memory that are affected, whereas procedural memory remains relatively intact. Procedural memory—which comprises well-established skills, such as driving a car—is unscathed because it doesn't depend on the hippocampus or other brain structures damaged by amnesia. Steven, the patient I described in the beginning of this chapter, could recall the minute details of how to make a leather vest (a procedural memory) but could not remember newly encountered names or faces, or recent conversations (declarative memories).

People with amnesia can learn new skills. Studies in which patients with amnesia have spent time each day practicing new activities, such as playing computer games, show that their performance improves over time and with practice—an indication that they are capable of acquiring new procedural memories. But these patients typically have no recall of having played or even having seen the computer games that they've been practicing. This phenomenon has been termed learning without awareness.

Organic Amnesia

Amnesia can occur as a result of damage to the medial temporal lobes (hippocampus) or diencephalon (thalamus). Causes of medial temporal amnesia include temporary disruption of oxygen flow to the brain, stroke of the posterior cerebral artery, certain

Common Causes of Amnesia

Traumatic brain injury

Korsakoff's syndrome (thiamine deficiency associated with chronic alcoholism)

Viral encephalitis

Anoxia or hypoxia

Surgery on the temporal lobes of the brain to control epilepsy

Blockage of the posterior cerebral artery

Rupture or clipping of the anterior communicating artery (surgery for aneurysm)

Paraneoplastic limbic encephalitis (associated with cancer)

kinds of brain infections (such as viral encephalitis), and paraneoplastic limbic encephalitis associated with cancer. People with medial temporal amnesia forget information very soon after encountering it but generally have intact attention, insight, and overall intellectual function.

Electroconvulsive therapy (ECT) for severe depression can cause transient amnesia by disturbing the function of medial temporal structures. But ECT does not permanently damage the structures and the amnesia tends to diminish over time.

Diencephalic amnesia can be caused by Korsakoff's syndrome (the result of a thiamine deficiency associated with chronic alcoholism), as well as by other nutritional deficiencies, traumatic brain injury, stroke, or a tumor that damages the thalamus. This type of amnesia includes deficits in executive function and insight.

Transient Global Amnesia (TGA)

This is a rare syndrome in which a person has a short-lived episode of amnesia, usually lasting just a few hours and no longer than one day. The cause of TGA is unknown; it is not associated with any neurological signs or obvious neuropsychological deficit.

TGA is a transient inability to form new memories, as well as to recall memories from the days, weeks, or years prior to the onset. The person behaves normally and can talk, reason, and carry out other cognitive functions without obvious problem, but he or she can't remember anything that occurred during the episode. As the TGA resolves, the person recovers most memory function but has a persisting amnesia for events that occurred during the episode.

TGA typically occurs in people ages fifty and older. Although migraine, temporal lobe seizures, and transient ischemic attacks have been cited as possible causes, compelling evidence is lacking. Certain medicines have also been implicated, including sleeping medications and sedative hypnotics. One provocative causal hypothesis concerns transient reduction of blood flow to the medial temporal lobes or thalamus, structures critical for memory function. This type of reduced perfusion can occur with physical and emotional stress, when normal blood flow is partially diverted to other areas of the body. Reported trigger events include pain, physical exertion, cold water exposure, severe emotional stress, and sexual intercourse.

In a 2004 study published in *Neurology*, researchers studied thirty-one consecutive cases of TGA and found punctate (tiny) lesions in the hippocampus in twenty-six cases. They point out that although only two patients had MRI abnormalities in the acute phase of the episode, lesions were visible in all twenty-six cases on MRIs obtained between twenty-four and forty-eight hours after onset. This finding provides very strong support for an ischemic etiology in TGA.

Psychogenic Amnesia

In contrast to organic amnesia, psychogenic amnesia is caused by severe emotional trauma and does not entail structural brain injury. People with psychogenic amnesia exhibit a retrograde amnesia in which they lose memory for past events and previously known facts but are able to learn new information normally. Fugue state is a dramatic form of psychogenic amnesia in which an individual abruptly relocates to another city or region, assumes a new identity, and has no apparent memory of his or her previous life.

Psychogenic amnesia occasionally conveys psychological protection to the sufferer, walling off memory of unbearable trauma. Sigmund Freud described the defense mechanism of repression, in which disturbing thoughts or experiences are effectively forgotten by being relegated to the unconscious. As discussed in Chapter 3, the recovery of repressed memory has been a highly controversial issue in cases of suspected childhood abuse.

In other instances, retrograde amnesia is faked, apparently to serve a more nefarious purpose. Malingered amnesia may constitute an attempt to elude responsibility for moral or criminal wrongdoing.

Hollywood Amnesia

The scene opens with a grainy black-and-white wide-angle shot of a nondescript ramshackle motel. The wind picks up, raising a cloud of dust and sending tumbleweed careening across the parking lot. Cut to an interior shot of one of the rooms. A middle-aged man with three days of beard stubble gazes into the bathroom mirror, rubbing a bruise on his forehead. The man's thoughts are heard in a voiceover: "Where am I? How did I get here? *Who* am I?"

He opens a closet door and gasps as the camera pans down to the motionless body of a beautiful young woman. In the next sequence, the panicked man is seen searching through the parking lot, trying to match the key tag he found in his pocket with the license plate of one of the cars parked in the lot. He finds the car, gets in, and drives off at high speed.

Cinematic depictions of amnesia can be quite dramatic—and scientifically implausible. The notion that a blow to the head can

The Case of HM

Scientists learned a lot about the neuroanatomy of memory and amnesia more than half a century ago from the case of a young man in Connecticut (now famous in the medical literature as HM) who underwent brain surgery for relief from epileptic seizures. Taking desperate measures to stop the seizures, a Yale surgeon removed large portions of both medial temporal lobes, including the hippocampus, the amygdala, and the entorhinal and perirhinal cortices. The surgery controlled HM's epilepsy, but it left him with profound amnesia.

Although his procedural memory and his memory for events prior to the surgery were largely unaffected, HM was unable to learn new factual information or create new episodic memories. He described his experience in the following words: "Right now, I'm wondering, have I done or said anything amiss? You see, at this moment everything looks clear to me, but what happened just before? That's what worries me. It's like waking from a dream. I just don't remember."

erase the most central aspects of personal identity while sparing general functional capacity makes for an intriguing movie plot but does not make neurological sense.

In real life, people with amnesia caused by a concussive injury don't forget everything. They retain their general level of intelligence and a normal span of attention. They can form short-term memories lasting perhaps a few minutes, provided that there is no intervening interference. The breakdown primarily occurs with new fact learning and recall of episodic memories, which are formed and stored by the affected structures.

Treatment for Amnesia

There's no specific treatment for amnesia, but depending on the cause, the symptoms often improve over time. If the amnesia results from a mild concussion, most of the lost memory will gradually return. In more severe traumatic brain injuries, the reinstatement of memory for events that occurred prior to the injury is referred to as a shrinking retrograde amnesia. However, memories formed just before and soon after the damage occurred are usually lost forever. The more severe the traumatic brain injury, the more significant the degree of persistent memory impairment.

With other causes of amnesia, the prospects for improvement also depend on the severity of the problem. Once a patient with thiamine deficiency and chronic alcoholism has crossed the threshold into Korsakoff's syndrome, deficits tend to be enduring. However, people with alcohol-related memory impairment that has not progressed to Korsakoff's can regain a substantial degree of memory function if they stop consuming alcohol, improve their diet, and remediate vitamin deficiency.

People with psychogenic amnesia can recover their memory function, sometimes with the help of psychotherapy that supports self-awareness and insight. But as I discussed in Chapter 3, the concept of recovered memories is controversial. There are legions of quack practitioners who claim to have recovered repressed memories using a heavy-handed, agenda-driven approach when in fact they probably created and implanted ten false traumatic memories for every one bona fide recovered memory.

Mild Cognitive Impairment

In recent years, the distinction between normal age-related memory loss and abnormal cognitive function has blurred as researchers have focused on a particular group of older people: they have memory problems that exceed those seen in normal aging but not of sufficient severity to warrant a diagnosis of dementia. These people have mild cognitive impairment, the loss of a single mental function—usually memory—that is more persistent and severe than is seen in normal aging. All other cognitive functions are normal.

Experts disagree regarding exactly how to think about mild cognitive impairment. One perspective is that it represents a potential transitional state between normal cognitive function and dementia. Another viewpoint dismisses the notion of mild cognitive impairment, simply regarding the symptoms as constituting very early Alzheimer's disease. But we do know that the disorder becomes more common with age.

One key difference between normal memory loss and mild cognitive impairment might be the nature of the information that is forgotten. With normal memory loss, you have difficulty recalling inconsequential information, such as the name of a casual acquaintance or the deadline for renewing a magazine subscription. With mild cognitive impairment, you're more likely to forget information that matters to you, such as the names of close friends or the dates of family members' birthdays that you used to know.

On clinical memory tests, people with mild cognitive impairment have trouble remembering the details of pictures that they saw or paragraphs they read just a few minutes earlier. Their memory difficulty is comparable to that of someone with very mild Alzheimer's disease. But unlike a patient with very early Alzheimer's disease, their performance is normal on tests that measure other aspects of cognition, such as attention, language, spatial construction, and executive function. Furthermore, their ability to function in everyday life at home and work remains substantially intact.

For years, we wondered whether mild cognitive impairment was a precursor to Alzheimer's disease. It now appears that it often is. Studies show that the risk of developing Alzheimer's disease is much higher for people with mild cognitive impairment than for people with normal age-related memory loss. According to an analysis of several studies, 6 percent of people ages sixty-five to sixty-nine with a diagnosis of mild cognitive impairment progressed to a diagnosis of Alzheimer's disease per year compared with just 0.2 percent of people in this age range in the general population. And 25 percent of people ages eighty-five to eighty-nine with mild cognitive impairment progressed to Alzheimer's disease each year compared with just 4 percent of people this age in the general population.

But this isn't to say that every person with mild cognitive impairment is destined to develop Alzheimer's disease. Some people with mild cognitive impairment exhibit no further decline for several years, and some even improve. One study followed people with mild cognitive impairment for three years, during which time 81 percent did not develop Alzheimer's disease. Of that large majority, 29 percent experienced no further deterioration, and 15 percent actually improved during the study period. In a study presented at the 2003 meeting of the American Neurological Association, researchers reported that 27 percent of people with mild cognitive impairment remained cognitively stable for an average of twelve years.

Researchers continue to study the relationship between mild cognitive impairment and Alzheimer's disease. A crucial question is whether treating mild cognitive impairment with certain medicines can prevent the conversion to Alzheimer's disease. The National Institute on Aging studied the ability of donepezil (Aricept), one of the drugs approved for treating Alzheimer's disease, to prevent progression to dementia in people diagnosed with mild cognitive impairment. Over the first half of the three-year study period, people who received donepezil were less likely to progress to a dementia diagnosis than people who had been randomized to the placebo condition. As we learn more about mild cognitive

Diagnostic Criteria for Mild Cognitive Impairment

Subjective memory complaint

Objective evidence of memory impairment on formal neuropsychological testing

Normal general cognitive function

Intact activities of daily living

No dementia

impairment and develop more effective treatments for Alzheimer's disease, preventive therapies are bound to become available for individuals who are at increased risk for both disorders.

Dementia

Dementia is a progressive deterioration of memory and other cognitive functions. Although extremely rare in people younger than sixty years old, dementia becomes increasingly more common with age. The incidence is about 10 percent at age sixty-five and doubles every ten years thereafter. The leading cause of dementia is Alzheimer's disease; other causes include cerebrovascular disease, Lewy-body disease, Parkinson's disease, alcoholism, HIV, and rare degenerative brain disorders, such as Pick's disease, progressive supranuclear palsy, Creutzfeldt-Jakob disease, and Huntington's disease.

In addition to advancing age, factors that increase the risk of developing dementia are a family history of Alzheimer's disease, possession of the e4 ApoE allele (a genetic variant that increases the risk of Alzheimer's disease), traumatic brain injury, and exposure to toxic substances. Some new research suggests a causal role for certain types of viral infections, including herpes simplex virus type 1 and chlamydia, but these findings remain highly controversial.

Although people in the earliest stages of dementia often sense that something is wrong, the illness eventually robs them of the insight needed to appreciate their problem. Consequently, it's usually up to a family member or friend to recognize the symptoms. If you suspect that someone you know has dementia, arrange for a medical evaluation.

Doctors diagnose dementia by examining a person's behavior and cognitive function, as well as by gathering evidence from brain imaging studies and other laboratory tests, as I discussed in Chapter 6. The workup will consider possible reversible forms of dementia—for example, normal pressure hydrocephalus, which can be treated surgically, or chronic vitamin B_{12} deficiency, which can be managed with regular injections of the vitamin.

Though some forms of dementia are reversible, many aren't. There are several medications for memory dysfunction associated with dementia that can bring about temporary, mild improvements and delay symptom progression. I discuss these medications in Chapter 8.

Alzheimer's Disease

Alzheimer's disease is the leading cause of dementia, accounting for between 50 and 70 percent of all cases. The outward signs of classical Alzheimer's disease are all too familiar: the insidious onset of memory dysfunction that relentlessly worsens over time and comes to eclipse all aspects of cognitive function. Less frequently, the initial symptoms may be in another neuropsychological realm, such as word finding, higher-order visual processing, spatial construction, or executive function. Patients with Alzheimer's disease also exhibit changes in personality and a decline in self-care. Inside the brain, the neuropathological features of Alzheimer's disease are a significant loss of neurons and the accumulation of amyloid "plaques" and neurofibrillary "tangles."

In the early stages, pathological features are concentrated in the hippocampus and other regions of the brain that are important for memory consolidation. Long-term memory is often spared in people with mild to moderate Alzheimer's disease; many can recall events and facts from years ago in great detail. But as Alzheimer's disease progresses and extends to other areas of the cortex, long-term memory breaks down, too. The brain atrophies (shrinks), particularly in the temporal and parietal regions, as you can see in Figure 7.1, which compares the brain of someone who had Alzheimer's disease with the brain of someone about the same age who did not have Alzheimer's. People with Alzheimer's disease are also vulnerable to the development of psychiatric symptoms including depression, agitation, hallucinations, and delusions.

Alzheimer's disease becomes dramatically more common with age. The incidence is just 3 percent among Americans ages sixty-five to seventy-four, but it climbs to 47 percent of Americans ages eighty-five and older, as shown in Figure 7.2.

FIGURE 7.1 Comparison of Normal Brain and One with Alzheimer's Disease

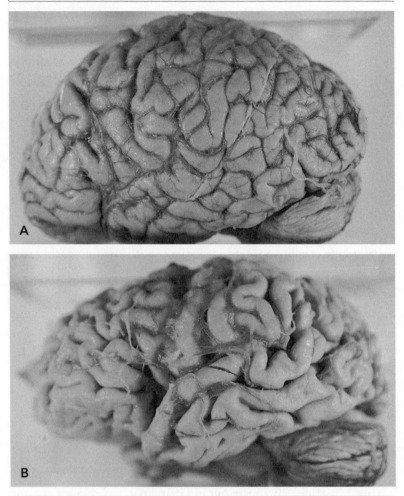

A. Normal elderly brain. B. Elderly brain with Alzheimer's disease. By Cecil Runyons, Sanders-Brown Center on Aging, University of Kentucky. Used with permission.

Vascular Dementia

The second leading cause of dementia, vascular dementia is the result of one or more strokes that interrupt blood flow to the brain. The lack of perfusion damages neurons by starving them of oxygen. In contrast to Alzheimer's disease, which commences

FIGURE 7.2 Risk of Alzheimer's Disease by Age

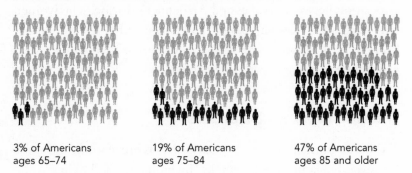

3% of Americans
ages 65–74

19% of Americans
ages 75–84

47% of Americans
ages 85 and older

gradually, vascular dementia often starts suddenly—right after a stroke—and then progresses in a stepwise fashion, with further declines in function resulting from subsequent small strokes or cumulative cerebrovascular compromise.

You can reduce the risk of vascular dementia by taking steps to control the conditions that can lead to stroke—hypertension, heart disease, diabetes, and obesity—as well as by not smoking. There are medications available, such as aspirin and warfarin, that can improve cerebral blood flow and possibly help prevent further memory deterioration following a stroke.

Mixed Dementia

Mixed dementia refers to a syndrome with underlying pathological features of both Alzheimer's disease and vascular dementia. The diagnosis is often made in someone with symptoms of dementia who has a personal history of vascular risk factors and a family history of Alzheimer's disease.

The link between vascular dementia and Alzheimer's disease may be more than just a coincidence; research suggests that vascular problems play a role in the development of Alzheimer's. A study published in the *Archives of Neurology* in 2003 found that adults who'd had strokes were at higher risk of developing Alzheimer's disease than people without a history of stroke. This finding added weight to an earlier, well-known National Institute on Aging–funded study involving 678 nuns that uncovered an association between strokes and Alzheimer's disease. The women who had had strokes plus plaque and tangle pathology were more likely to be diagnosed with Alzheimer's disease than women who had plaque and tangle pathology alone.

Treating Memory Disorders

The best treatment for memory disorders is prevention, and there are several measures you can take, including the following:

- **Protect your head.** A significant blow to the head can cause memory impairment and increase the risk of future dementia. Wear a seat belt when in a motor vehicle to guard against a head injury from a traffic accident. Wear a helmet when bike riding, skiing, or in-line skating. Use a protective mouth guard and appropriate head gear when playing contact sports.
- **Protect your blood vessels.** A blockage in a blood vessel to the brain can cause a stroke, which can lead to dementia. Reduce your risk of stroke by exercising regularly, maintaining a normal weight, and not smoking.
- **Control high blood pressure and high cholesterol.** These problems can also lead to stroke. Treating them with medications or behavioral strategies (such as exercise and a healthy diet) can help guard against stroke and, therefore, dementia.

Though we do not currently have definitive treatments for mild cognitive impairment and most forms of dementia, several drugs are available that can diminish the symptoms for a period of time. I discuss these medications, as well as new drugs under study, in the next chapter.

CHAPTER 8

Memory Medications

The search for medications that can renew a fading memory or enhance a normal one has been gathering momentum at a geometric pace for more than a decade, ever since the FDA approved tacrine (Cognex), the first drug for the treatment of Alzheimer's disease. There is not yet a pill proven to conquer age-related memory loss, although there is certainly no shortage of herbal preparations that make this claim. There are a growing number of FDA-approved medications for the symptomatic treatment of memory disorders. An even larger number of candidates are in the drug-development pipeline.

Currently available drugs can slightly improve symptoms and temporarily slow the progress of dementia; these drugs are being prescribed more and more frequently for mild cognitive impairment. Importantly, supplements of vitamin E are also helpful—about as effective for Alzheimer's disease as the prescription drugs. However, as of now, we don't have a medication that can cure any of these memory disorders or reverse the course of the neuronal damage that they cause.

Many pharmaceutical companies are making use of the wealth of new findings on the biology of Alzheimer's disease to develop medications that, ideally, will halt this memory disorder by tar-

133

How Memory Drugs Work

The drugs now used to treat dementia and mild cognitive impairment work by altering the activity and availability of neurotransmitters in the brain that play a key role in memory. Most currently approved drugs increase the availability of acetylcholine, a key neurotransmitter involved in memory function. These drugs, called cholinesterase inhibitors, include donepezil (Aricept), galantamine (Reminyl), rivastigmine (Exelon), and tacrine (Cognex).

While they are generally equally effective, the cholinesterase inhibitors differ in their convenience of use and their side effects. Donepezil is the most convenient of the drugs because it's taken just once a day, whereas the others have to be taken twice a day. The most common side effects of cholinesterase inhibitors are gastrointestinal symptoms, including nausea and diarrhea, with decreased appetite and weight loss. Despite the fact that all of these medications are of the same class, some people occasionally develop side effects to one but not to another. Tacrine, the oldest of the drugs, is rarely prescribed anymore because it has the most severe side effects—it can cause liver damage.

A newer drug, called memantine (Namenda), relies on a different mode of action. Memantine is an NMDA (N-methyl-D-aspartate) receptor antagonist, which blocks glutamate, another neurotransmitter, from latching onto NMDA receptors. Receptors are sites on neurons that receive specific neurotransmitters. Although the precise mechanism of memantine's beneficial effect is unclear, it may be that blocking NMDA receptors prevents overstimulation by excessive levels of glutamate that can be toxic to neurons and synapses, leading to memory loss and problems with other brain functions. The most common side effects reported with memantine include dizziness, confusion, headache, and constipation.

geting the underlying pathology. I feel optimistic that disease-modifying therapy is on the horizon.

Drugs for Alzheimer's Disease

Currently available medications can reduce the symptoms of Alzheimer's disease in some individuals and delay the progression of symptoms by a number of months, thereby prolonging the amount of time that patients can remain independent. The cholinesterase inhibitors and vitamin E are prescribed for people with mild to moderate Alzheimer's disease; memantine is helpful for people with moderate to severe disease.

Medications for Mild to Moderate Alzheimer's Disease

All of the cholinesterase inhibitors are equally effective in temporarily stabilizing memory and other functions of people in the early to middle stage of Alzheimer's disease, although people's response is highly individual. People who aren't helped by one of the drugs might respond to one of the others.

After using one of the cholinesterase inhibitors for several weeks, about half of patients are somewhat more alert and better able to care for themselves and engage in activities. The drugs may have other benefits, according to a 2003 report in the *Journal of the American Medical Association*. This review of twenty-nine studies found that cholinesterase inhibitors might also ease some of the psychiatric symptoms of Alzheimer's disease, such as depression, anxiety, hallucinations, and delusions.

Treatment for Moderate to Severe Alzheimer's Disease

Memantine, either alone or in combination with one of the cholinesterase inhibitors, is used for patients with moderate to severe Alzheimer's disease. Research shows that memantine helps slow the progression of memory loss and other cognitive symptoms for a period of time. A study published in the *Journal of the American Medical Association* in 2004 compared a group of Alzheimer's disease patients taking donepezil plus memantine with another group, taking donepezil plus a placebo. People taking both medications for six months exhibited a significantly slower pace of decline in cognitive functions. A similar finding was reported with respect to activities of daily living, which refer to bathing, dressing, and other aspects of personal care. Although patients in both groups declined over the six-month study, the decline was steeper in the donepezil plus placebo group.

Our clinical experience with memantine is similar to what we see with the cholinesterase inhibitors. Specifically, memantine appears to temporarily slow symptom progression but has no effect on the underlying disease process and does not alter the overall outcome of Alzheimer's disease.

Ginkgo Biloba. Several small studies have found that an extract from the nuts and leaves of the ginkgo biloba tree is somewhat beneficial to people with moderate to severe Alzheimer's disease— comparable to the benefits from vitamin E and the memory drugs. The mechanism of action of the gingko extract, known as EGb 761, is believed to relate to its antioxidant properties. There's some evidence that ginkgo might help prevent the formation of beta-amyloid in the brain, a key pathological feature and the possible cause of Alzheimer's disease.

Herbal supplements containing ginkgo are sold over the counter and marketed widely as memory enhancers. However, a 2002 study with cognitively normal elderly individuals failed to demonstrate a benefit on multiple measures of memory function. A larger, multicenter study is ongoing that uses higher doses of EGb 761 with cognitively normal people.

As is the case with any of the herbal remedies and other *nutraceuticals* (food supplements thought to have medicinal properties), I caution my patients and their families that because herbal supplements aren't subject to FDA scrutiny, there's no way to know the exact content, composition, or purity of the product they are buying. Because findings from clinical trials of these compounds are based on precise quantities of active ingredients, they might not pertain to you if you happen to purchase a product with a different composition. Furthermore, information used to substantiate claims of efficacy in the marketing of these substances is rarely based on the same caliber of rigorous scientific methodology required by the FDA.

Drugs for Mild Cognitive Impairment

Medications used for Alzheimer's disease appear to improve alertness, attentiveness, and memory performance in people with mild cognitive impairment. There is also evidence that they have the potential to forestall progression from mild cognitive impairment to Alzheimer's disease, at least temporarily.

In a study of 269 people with mild cognitive impairment, 61 percent of those who took donepezil for six months had improved memory function compared with 50 percent of patients in a placebo control group. In 2004 a Mayo Clinic study of 769 people with mild cognitive impairment reported that those who took donepezil for eighteen months were less likely to develop Alzheimer's disease than those taking either vitamin E or a placebo. After eighteen months, however, the likelihood of converting to Alzheimer's disease was the same for all three groups. Donepezil seemed to delay the onset of Alzheimer's by about six months. Rivastigmine has yielded similar results in recent research.

Medications that have been used to boost levels of the neurotransmitter dopamine in the treatment of Parkinson's disease are also being investigated for treating mild cognitive impairment. Such drugs are used in other countries but are not yet approved for this specific indication in the United States. Clinical trials have found that one such drug, called piribedil (Trivastal), slowed cognitive decline for at least several months.

Drugs for Vascular Dementia or Mixed Dementia

Treatment of these types of dementia is two-pronged. First, we aim to prevent further injury to the brain by controlling vascular problems—the root cause of vascular dementia and one of the causes of mixed dementia. This means managing hypertension, high cholesterol, and diabetes with a healthier diet, more exercise, and, if necessary, medications.

Second, we treat symptoms of vascular dementia with the same medications that are approved for Alzheimer's disease. Clinical trials have found that galantamine, donepezil, and memantine bring about temporary improvements in memory and related cognitive domains, as well as in daily functioning in patients with vascular dementia.

Alternative Remedies for Memory Loss

Several colleagues at Harvard in the Division of Complementary and Alternative Medicine conduct research on therapies outside of mainstream American medicine for preventing and treating health problems. These doctors are curious about herbs, homeopathic medicines, and other products typically sold in health food stores, as well as natural approaches to healing that are used in cultures around the world. They have researched a number of substances that claim to improve memory, but so far these investigations have not yielded compelling supportive evidence.

Most of the products tested don't get into the nervous system because they're broken down during digestion. If they don't reach the nervous system, they can't affect memory. One possible exception has been ginkgo biloba, which seems potentially helpful to peo-

Can Memory Drugs Enhance Normal Memory?

If medications for Alzheimer's disease can improve memory and related cognitive function in people with the disorder, can they confer the same benefits to people with normal memory? The answer is, maybe.

A 2001 study compared the performance of a small cohort of commercial airline pilots who took donepezil for one month with those who took a placebo. The pilots who took the Alzheimer's disease drug performed better on difficult flight-simulation tasks. The researchers interpreted the results to mean that donepezil might have improved the pilots' procedural memory—their retention and execution of complex skills.

But we still know very little about the effects of memory medications on healthy people. Although memory drugs have been proven safe for people with memory disorders, they might cause unforeseen effects in the brains of healthy people when used over an extended period of time. In addition, these drugs are expensive and can have rugged side effects, which seem like a big price to pay for some potential marginal benefit.

Studies are under way to see if these and other medicines are truly "smart drugs," able to safely help sharpen anybody's mind and enhance cognitive performance. Even if they are effective, there are many legal and ethical issues to consider. For example, what if only the wealthy can afford them—wouldn't this give their children an unfair advantage in school or when competing for jobs as adults? Should your employer have the right to require you to take a medication that would improve your performance on the job? I discuss some of the ethical and social challenges posed by the emerging trend toward cognitive enhancers in Chapter 11.

ple with Alzheimer's disease, although not for people with normal age-related memory loss.

There may well be other herbs and supplements that can improve memory, but scientific research hasn't yet identified them. Therefore, I recommend saving your money and relying on the scientifically proven therapies and techniques discussed in this book.

New Drugs Under Study

There are many compounds under development for treating Alzheimer's disease and other memory disorders. Some of the experimental compounds work on the same principle as the medications available today. But several others work in completely different ways and hold the potential of actually preventing or reversing dementia and other memory disorders. I join other memory doctors and our patients in the hope (and expectation) that one or more of these new medications will yield greater benefits than the drugs we have today.

Keep in mind that drug development research focuses on two levels of effect: physiological and behavioral. Physiological effect is the capacity of a drug to alter some underlying biological marker or process. In other words, if a researcher hypothesizes that drug X will clear beta-amyloid from the brain of a patient with Alzheimer's disease, does the study in fact demonstrate that the drug has accomplished this? Behavioral effect refers to the capacity of the drug to make a significant difference in a relevant, measurable aspect of a person's functioning. In other words, does drug X actually improve memory function as reflected in a score on a memory test?

Even if drug X is physiologically effective, it may fail to produce a behavioral change. This type of result may lead the drug developer to question the assumption that the drug is targeting the relevant physiological disease factor. Alternatively, it may mean that behavioral efficacy might only be realized with higher doses or when therapeutic intervention occurs at an earlier stage of the disease.

Medications for Alzheimer's disease and other memory disorders can be divided into three broad categories, based on their effects and on the groups of people who stand to benefit from them. Many of the investigational drugs fit into more than one of these categories. Following is a rundown of current research.

Symptomatic Stabilization or Improvement

This category includes drugs that affect only the symptoms of memory disorders, not their causes. The FDA-approved drugs we have now (the cholinesterase inhibitors and memantine) fall into this category. They are intended for people with Alzheimer's disease, vascular and mixed dementia, and mild cognitive impairment. Other compounds aimed at symptomatic therapy include the following:

- **Huperzine A.** This is a naturally occurring cholinesterase inhibitor derived from a Chinese herb and widely used to treat Alzheimer's disease in China. Huperzine A may be more potent than donepezil, and there is some speculation that it may also convey a neuroprotective effect. The National Institute on Aging is sponsoring a clinical trial to assess its safety and effectiveness.
- **AMPA receptor potentiators (ampakines).** Ampakines accelerate communication between neurons. The hope is that they can function somewhat like an amplifier, making neurons more receptive to incoming information and thus better able to encode it into memory. Small clinical trials with one ampakine drug (Ampalex, also known as CX516) determined that it was safe and that it had the expected physiological effect in the brain. But it remains to be seen if this effect is powerful enough to actually improve memory

function. A larger clinical trial is ongoing at the National Institutes of Health.

- **Calcium channel modulators.** This is a new drug category, aimed at decreasing calcium influx into neurons. (Do not confuse calcium channel *modulators* with the calcium channel *blockers*, a frequently prescribed class of drugs used in the management of angina, hypertension, and cardiac arrhythmias.) Although calcium–related wear and tear is a normal effect of aging, excess calcium can damage neurons and contribute to memory disorders. Clinical trials are testing a calcium channel modulator in people with Alzheimer's disease, mild cognitive impairment, and vascular dementia. This compound would regulate the amount of calcium flowing through the neuronal channel, allowing enough through to maintain normal function while preventing neurotoxic levels. If the drug works as intended, neurons would maintain optimal responsiveness to incoming information and signals.

- **Drugs that maintain cyclic AMP.** Cyclic AMP (cAMP) is a type of neurotransmitter known as a chemical secondary messenger. Cyclic AMP activates a protein called CREB, which switches on genes that affect the release of other neurotransmitters involved in memory consolidation and retrieval. A number of drugs being developed aim to augment brain levels of cAMP in people with Alzheimer's disease and mild cognitive impairment.

- **Nicotine.** Though smoking is unquestionably bad for memory and other aspects of health, nicotine by itself has been found to mimic the function of acetylcholine, a key neurotransmitter involved in memory, which is depleted in Alzheimer's disease. An ongoing study at the National Institute on Aging is researching the ability of nicotine (via the nicotine patch) to improve cognitive symptoms in mild cognitive impairment and reduce progression from mild cognitive impairment to Alzheimer's disease.

Disease Modification

Medications in this category are designed to attack the underlying neuropathological features of Alzheimer's disease, thereby halting disease progression and either preventing further symptom progression or reversing symptoms that have already been established. The most common targets of disease-modification strategies for Alzheimer's disease are the two primary neuropathological features: beta-amyloid, which forms amyloid plaques, and tau, the primary constituent of neurofibrillary tangles.

- **Alzhemed.** This compound is believed to work by binding to beta-amyloid while it is still in a soluble form, thereby preventing it from transitioning to the "sticky" form it assumes when it aggregates into plaques. Alzhemed also may achieve some effect through an anti-inflammatory mechanism. In a multicenter clinical trial begun in 2004, Alzhemed has shown promise in stabilizing symptoms in people with mild to moderate Alzheimer's disease.
- **Clioquinol.** Clioquinol (iodochlorhydroxyquin) is an old-line antibiotic that has recently shown potential promise in the treatment of Alzheimer's disease. Clioquinol appears to work by extracting metals (zinc and copper) from beta-amyloid, thereby effectively "disassembling" amyloid plaques. Clioquinol also appears to decrease the production of hydrogen peroxide, which is toxic to neurons.
- **Alzheimer's disease vaccine.** Traditional vaccines in humans are used to provoke the production of specialized proteins called antibodies, our natural defenses against pathogens. There is reason to believe that a vaccine can be a weapon against Alzheimer's disease. This hope was raised by the finding that the human immune system contains antibodies against beta-amyloid protein.

   A 1999 landmark study reported on the development of an injectable vaccine (AN-1792), which successfully cleared Alzheimer's pathology in mice that were genetically engineered to have high levels of human brain beta-amyloid. Clinical trials initiated in 2001 with 372 humans from twenty-eight study sites were discontinued in January 2002 after four subjects developed encephalitis, a potentially fatal brain inflammatory response. Ultimately, 6 percent of the research sample developed symptoms or had other findings associated with encephalitis.

One of the people who developed encephalitis later died from an unrelated cause (pulmonary embolism). However, a brain autopsy revealed that AN-1792 had successfully cleared much of the Alzheimer's pathology in the same way as had been demonstrated in earlier animal research. Although researchers must remain cautious about drawing conclusions from a single case, this finding implies that a robust immunological response had occurred and was dramatically effective on the physiological level.

In another report, published in 2003, researchers at one of the clinical trial sites in Switzerland reported that analysis of their thirty patients suggested that immunization had slowed disease progression. Again, caution must be exercised in drawing general conclusions from these data. Nevertheless, the findings have generated a good deal of excitement and optimism, and a number of different research groups are now working on a second generation of modified "passive" immunization strategies.

- **Lithium–like drugs.** Long used to treat bipolar disorder (manic–depressive illness), lithium is being studied for its potential to treat Alzheimer's disease. In animal research, lithium has been found to block an enzyme (glycogen synthase kinase) that is essential to the formation of beta-amyloid plaques. Lithium also appears to interfere with the production of the tau protein, another suspected pathological feature of Alzheimer's disease.

  However, even if lithium has the same beneficial effect in humans, it's doubtful that it would constitute a practical treatment for Alzheimer's disease because it can produce a number of side effects, and elderly people would be especially vulnerable to them. But other drugs might be developed that inhibit the Alzheimer's process in the same way as lithium.

- **Secretase inhibitors.** Gamma- and beta-secretase are enzymes that detach the beta-amyloid segment from a larger protein, effectively putting it into position to begin the process of aggregating into plaques. Compounds that inhibit these enzymes have become an intense focus of research as potential disease-modifying agents, although none have yet advanced to actual treatment studies.

- **Phenserine.** Phenserine is a new cholinesterase inhibitor currently in advanced clinical trials that is purported to have both symptomatic and potential disease-modifying effects, which can slow the progression of Alzheimer's disease. Researchers say that it has demonstrated the ability to inhibit formation of the amyloid precursor protein, the source of beta-amyloid.

Disease Prevention

The goal here is to prevent occurrence of disease and symptoms in individuals presumed to be at high risk for the development of Alzheimer's disease or mild cognitive impairment. For this approach to work, we would need both a reliable method or marker for identifying at-risk individuals *and* therapies that can effectively prevent the disease from developing.

Although we know that the pathological cascade that eventually causes Alzheimer's disease begins decades before symptoms appear, we do not yet possess an early preclinical marker. Performance on neuropsychological tests has thus far been the most sensitive index; subtle changes on specialized imaging studies are being further investigated. Ultimately, the treatment of Alzheimer's disease will occur when an at-risk individual is in his or her twenties, thirties, or forties. Studies are looking at whether the following substances can prevent and, in some cases, modify the Alzheimer's disease process.

- **Antioxidants.** Vitamin E and vitamin C have established antioxidant properties, and vitamin E has been shown to ameliorate symptoms of Alzheimer's disease. A current large-scale study cosponsored by the National Institute on Aging and the National Cancer Institute is ongoing to determine if a combination of vitamin E and selenium also conveys a preventive benefit.

- **High-dose vitamins.** A multicenter clinical trial sponsored by the National Institute on Aging aims to find out if high-dose supplements of folate and vitamins B_6 and B_{12} can slow the progression of Alzheimer's disease. These vitamins appear to moderate blood levels of homocysteine, an amino acid that can damage delicate blood vessels and render a person more vulnerable to cerebrovascular disorders and Alzheimer's disease. I discussed homocysteine as a potential contributory factor in Alzheimer's disease and other forms of dementia in Chapter 5.

- **Nonsteroidal anti-inflammatory drugs (NSAIDs).** NSAIDs constitute a class of painkillers that includes ibuprofen (Advil, Motrin, and others), naproxen (Aleve, Anaprox, and others), and celecoxib (Celebrex). These medicines have been studied for their potential to prevent and treat Alzheimer's disease. Scientists also think that because these agents reduce inflammation throughout the body, they should be able to reduce the nerve cell inflammation that is associated with the disease. Hopes have also been raised by laboratory and animal studies showing that some of these drugs interfere with the production of beta-amyloid plaques.

    Findings have thus far been mixed. Epidemiological studies involving thousands of people have found that frequent use of NSAIDs seems to be associated with decreased likelihood of future development of Alzheimer's disease. Only two of these drugs—rofecoxib (Vioxx) and naproxen—have been tested as potential treatments for Alzheimer's disease, but they did not reduce or slow the progression of the symptoms. Rofecoxib was subsequently removed from the market because of dangerous cardiovascular side effects, including stroke and heart attack. Naproxen and celecoxib had been the focus of a large Alzheimer's disease prevention trial by the National Institutes of Health, which was suspended in 2004 after similar concerns were raised regarding cardiovascular side effects. The status of NSAIDs in the prevention of Alzheimer's disease remains unknown at present.

- **Statins.** Atorvastatin (Lipitor), simvastatin (Zocor), and pravastatin (Pravachol) belong to a commonly prescribed class of cholesterol-lowering medications called statins. Some preliminary research shows that taking statins can reduce the risk of Alzheimer's disease by as much as 70 percent and may also help prevent mild cognitive impairment. On the other hand, a Columbia University study published in 2004 found that people being treated with statins for hyperlipidemia did not have a lower risk of future development of either Alzheimer's disease or vascular dementia.

  A 2002 German study of forty-four people with Alzheimer's disease but normal levels of cholesterol examined the effect of simvastatin on beta-amyloid. After twenty-six weeks, people with mild Alzheimer's disease experienced a significant decrease in beta-amyloid concentration measured in the cerebrospinal fluid. However, there was no change in cerebrospinal fluid levels of beta-amyloid in people with moderate or severe disease. A current large multicenter study sponsored by the National Institute on Aging is investigating simvastatin as a treatment for slowing the progression of Alzheimer's disease.

It stands to reason that statins might help either prevent or treat Alzheimer's disease. We have abundant evidence of a relationship between cholesterol and the formation of beta-amyloid plaques; people with the ApoE e4 allele gene are at increased risk of hypercholesterolemia as well as Alzheimer's disease. We don't yet know enough about the efficacy of statins for the treatment of Alzheimer's disease to recommend that people take these drugs specifically to lower their risk of the disease. But in the meantime, if you have high cholesterol and are taking a statin to control it, you may realize a double benefit: lowering your cholesterol and reducing your risk of memory disorder.

- **Estrogen therapy.** Although recent large studies have found that hormone replacement therapy actually increases the risk of dementia in healthy postmenopausal women, there is some evidence that estrogen therapy may be helpful in the treatment of women with established Alzheimer's disease. One clinical trial is looking at raloxifene (Evista), an estrogen-like compound that is prescribed for osteoporosis and, unlike menopausal hormone therapy, is not associated with an increased risk of cancer and other illnesses. The purpose of the study is to determine if raloxifene can improve cognitive function and skills required for independent living in women with Alzheimer's disease. A trial sponsored by the National Institutes of Health is evaluating whether estrogen therapy, either alone or in combination with progestin, a synthetic hormone, can improve memory and related functions in postmenopausal women with mild to moderate Alzheimer's disease.

Improving Your Memory Without Medication

In addition to medications designed to help memory, there are many other practical, nonpharmacological strategies for improving one's memory. Some of these approaches can be effective for people with mild cognitive impairment and other memory disorders, as well as for people with age-related memory loss. I will describe various ways to protect and improve your memory in Chapters 9 and 10.

CHAPTER 9

Prevention and Proaction: The Path to Optimal Memory

No matter how old you are, it's not too late to take steps to prevent memory loss. In this chapter, I review thirteen strategies for achieving and maintaining optimal memory. Some are good health habits that can reduce the risk of illnesses that might impair your memory as well as the likelihood that you'll need medications with memory-related side effects. Others are strategies that appear to strengthen the brain and enhance cognitive function. Best of all, they're neither expensive nor difficult to carry out.

Obtain regular exercise

Put out the cigarettes

Take vitamins

Involve yourself with others

Maintain healthful nutrition

Aim for a good night's sleep

Learn something new

Moderate alcohol intake

Engage in life!

Manage stress

Organize your thinking, organize your life

Routinely take precautions to protect your brain

Yes you can! Maintain a positive attitude

The preventive measures described in this chapter have been scientifically studied and found to be highly effective in staving off age-related memory loss and reducing the risk of developing memory disorders.

Obtain Regular Exercise

Sound bodies *do* promote sound minds. People who engage in regular vigorous exercise tend to stay mentally sharp into their seventies and eighties and beyond. You don't have to run marathons or go to other extremes, but you should get your heart pumping faster and break a sweat. Participants in the MacArthur Foundation Study of Aging in America whose cognitive function remained strong were active almost daily. A 2000 study from the Case Western Reserve University School of Medicine concluded that people who exercised by walking or engaging in physically active hobbies, such as gardening, had a lower risk of Alzheimer's disease compared with people who were sedentary.

Why should physical exercise influence brain health and cognitive function? Researchers at the University of Illinois think the connection has to do with several factors, all bearing on the capacity of physical exercise to augment brain plasticity: increasing capillary growth around neurons, which provide blood-borne oxygen and nutrients; increasing synaptic density; and promoting positive cholinergic effects. These researchers published results of two studies in 2004.

The first study, of forty-one older adults, found that participants with higher cardiovascular fitness (as measured by maximum oxygen uptake during aerobic activity) performed better on a complex attentional task *and* demonstrated significantly greater fMRI activation in associated brain regions. In the second study, twenty-nine adults, ranging in age between fifty-eight and seventy-seven, were randomly assigned to either an aerobic exercise group or a control group that did stretching and toning. After six months, the aerobic group exhibited increased cardiovascular fitness (as evidenced by maximum oxygen uptake), better performance on the attentional task, and greater levels of task-related fMRI activation.

Physical activity has also been linked to a decreased risk of the development of dementia. Researchers in Hawaii found that older men who walked the least distance on a regular basis had an almost twofold increase in risk of developing dementia compared with men who walked the most. Harvard researchers reported a similar finding from the Nurses' Health Study, which has been following more than 120,000 American women since 1976.

I counsel my patients to build physical activity into their everyday routine. Many protest that it's hard to find the time to exercise, with their hectic work schedules and family obligations. My response is that, of course, some days it will be impossible to exercise. But don't let "I'm too busy" become an excuse to be sedentary. Here are some ways to get started being more physically active:

- When possible, walk or bicycle instead of driving or riding; jog instead of walking.
- Take a daily half-hour walk around the neighborhood in the evening or during your lunch break at work. For motivation, ask your spouse or a friend to walk with you.
- Use the stairs instead of the elevator.
- Consult a personal trainer to help you devise a home exercise routine combining aerobic exercise and weight training.
- Plant a garden.
- Take an exercise class or join a health club.
- Swim regularly if you have access to a pool or beach.
- Take up a sport that requires physical exertion, such as tennis, running, or cycling.

If you haven't been physically active recently, check with your doctor first.

Put Out the Cigarettes

Studies show that smokers don't remember as well as nonsmokers. That's no surprise when you consider that smoking is a risk factor for cardiovascular disease and other illnesses that contribute both directly and indirectly to memory loss. Smoking also damages the lungs and constricts blood vessels to the brain, depriving it of oxygen and possibly harming neurons.

British public health researchers have been following more than five thousand people born in 1946, surveying their smoking behavior at various times over the years. In 1999, when the subjects were fifty-three years old, the researchers explored the relationship between smoking status and performance on cognitive tests. Even when the data were controlled for sex, childhood cognitive ability (measured at age fifteen), educational achievement, and occupational class, the researchers found that smoking correlated with steeper declines on measures of verbal memory and visual processing speed. Importantly, they also found better cognitive performance among people who had stopped smoking during the study time frame.

A large European study reported similar findings in an elderly sample. Smokers exhibited a steeper rate of decline on a measure of global cognitive function than did nonsmokers. The researchers speculated that smoking might affect cognitive function by promoting cerebrovascular injury from atherosclerosis and hypertension.

Take Vitamins

I advise my patients to take vitamin C because the majority of the research suggests that antioxidants protect against memory loss due to aging and dementia, including Alzheimer's disease. Antioxidants combat free radicals, destructive molecules that occur naturally in the body and damage healthy tissue, including brain tissue. We know that free radicals accelerate the aging process, and therefore, it's reasonable to assume that they promote age-related memory loss. It's also likely that free radicals contribute to the development of Alzheimer's disease, because oxidative damage has been found on autopsy in the brains of Alzheimer's patients.

One study suggests that vitamins E and C are beneficial in the treatment of age-related memory loss. The 2002 study published in the *Archives of Neurology* suggested that vitamin E, but not the other antioxidants, may help slow the rate of age-related mental decline. Researchers surveyed 2,889 individuals (average age of seventy-four) with regard to nutritional intake and use of vitamin and mineral supplements and evaluated changes in cognitive function over an average of about three years. People who consumed the most vitamin E exhibited 36 percent less cognitive decline than those who consumed the least.

There's also evidence that vitamins C and E, taken together, might protect against dementia. A study of 3,385 Japanese American men ages seventy-one to ninety-three found that those who reported regular use of vitamin C and E supplements had an 88 percent lower incidence of vascular dementia compared with those who did not use the supplements. The rate of dementia was lowest among men who had taken vitamins C and E the longest, suggesting that long-term use is important for helping to preserve cognitive function over time.

Evidence bearing on the ability of antioxidant supplements to prevent Alzheimer's disease is mixed. A 2003 study of 980 people reported no association between antioxidant intake and later development of Alzheimer's disease. However, a larger 2004 study published in the *Archives of Neurology* found that people who used vitamin C and E supplements were less likely to develop Alzheimer's disease than those who didn't use these supplements. In this study, 4,740 people ages sixty-five and older were surveyed regarding vitamin use and evaluated for signs of Alzheimer's disease and other forms of dementia. The prevalence (number of cases of a disease in a given population *at a specific time*) of Alzheimer's disease was 78 percent lower among people who used vitamin C and E supplements than it was among those who did not. The incidence (rate of occurrence of new cases of a disease in a population *over a period of time*) of Alzheimer's disease during the course of the study was 64 percent lower in this group.

If you have problems with blood clotting—for instance, related to a vitamin K deficiency or if you take blood-thinning medication—you should check with your doctor before taking vitamin E because it can interfere with blood clotting.

As I discussed in Chapter 5, B vitamins (B_6, B_{12}, folic acid) are important for neuronal protection as well as the breakdown of homocysteine, an amino acid in the blood that, in high levels, is a major risk factor for heart disease, stroke, and peripheral vascular disease. Although sufficient levels of B vitamins are usually provided by a well-balanced diet, deficiencies tend to become more prevalent with age. You should work with your doctor to monitor your homocysteine level and correct vitamin B deficiencies with supplementation when necessary.

Involve Yourself with Others

It goes without saying that keeping up positive relationships with family and friends is emotionally and socially rewarding. But it's also good for your overall health and beneficial for your brain. The MacArthur study on aging and other research suggest that social support can improve mental performance.

A Canadian study published in 2003 sought to tease out the effect of social engagement on cognitive function in a group of people older than sixty-five. Over the course of four years, the researchers found that social ties were a strong predictor of cognitive functioning. In other words, the probability of maintaining strong cognitive function was highest among the elders who socialized often and had good social ties, and the probability of losing cognitive function was highest among participants who were not socially engaged. The researchers concluded that weak social ties and activity was a risk factor for cognitive decline.

There are several reasons that maintaining an active social life may help prevent memory loss. Interpersonal engagement may increase the likelihood of ongoing involvement in intellectually stimulating activities; I discuss the link between lifelong learning and preservation of cognitive function later in this chapter. Social connectedness also helps cushion the blow from stressful life events and therefore reduces the negative effect that stress can exert on the brain.

You might wonder if *all* social ties are good. In other words, should you mend fences with a disagreeable in-law or an annoying neighbor just because it might be good for you? Probably not, unless you think that the relationship is worth repairing. The best relationships are the ones you feel drawn to; they make you feel engaged, challenged, and supported.

Maintain Healthful Nutrition

When I encourage my patients to eat a healthy diet, I realize that most everyone has heard it all before. But when I tell them the ways in which some foods are good for the brain—and others are bad for the brain—they are more likely to pay attention.

Walter Willett's marvelous book *Eat, Drink, and Be Healthy* is a concise and persuasive state-of-the-art review of what you need to know to eat healthfully. Dr. Willett deconstructs the U.S. Department of Agriculture's Food Guide Pyramid and replaces it with his Healthy Eating Pyramid; a copy is taped to my refrigerator.

Eat plenty of fruits and vegetables, along with whole grains; obtain healthy fats from fish and nuts. These foods help keep your cholesterol levels in range and your arteries clear. These benefits in turn will decrease your risk of vascular disease and stroke, including strokes of the small "silent" variety that can cumulatively damage brain function. Fruits and vegetables can be beneficial in another way; many are good sources of antioxidants, nutrients that protect against age-related oxidative deterioration throughout the body, as well as B-complex vitamins. B vitamins

Brain Foods

Some foods can protect your memory by helping to prevent diseases that weaken the brain, whereas others can harm your memory by promoting those diseases.

- **Foods to eat.** Increase your consumption of fruits, vegetables, whole grains, nuts, and fish. These can reduce the risk of heart disease, stroke, and diabetes.
- **Foods to avoid.** Minimize your consumption of red meat, whole milk and other dairy products made with whole milk, and processed or packaged foods. These foods increase the risk of hypercholesterolemia, heart disease, and stroke.

are also found in whole-grain foods, rice, nuts, milk, eggs, meats, and fish.

Minimize your consumption of foods containing saturated fats or trans fats, which promote atherosclerosis, the accumulation of cholesterol and lipids on arterial walls. These fatty deposits, or plaques, result in the narrowing of blood vessels and can cause strokes if they detach and lodge in smaller blood vessels, blocking blood flow. Red meat and whole-milk dairy products are high in saturated fats. Many packaged foods and snacks contain partially hydrogenated oils and, therefore, tend to be high in trans fats. So be sure to read the labels!

Finally, eating healthfully means avoiding excess calories so that you can maintain a normal weight. Compared with people who are overweight, people whose weight is normal are less likely to develop age-related illnesses, such as adult-onset diabetes and hypertension, risk factors for cerebrovascular disease.

Aim for a Good Night's Sleep

Effective memory consolidation depends on sufficient quality sleep. Although people vary widely in the amount of sleep that they need, most adults require an average of approximately seven and a half hours per night. Research suggests that six hours of sleep at night is the minimum that most people need in order to be sufficiently alert the next day to maintain optimal memory. As important as the amount of sleep you get is the quality of your sleep. If you have sleep-related breathing problems, such as obstructive sleep apnea, you can sleep for ten hours a night and still not feel refreshed in the morning. If you think that you have sleep apnea (perhaps because your partner complains that you snore), it's essential that you see your doctor and have it treated.

Insomnia (chronic sleeplessness) is the most common sleep disorder, and it becomes more common with age. Approximately one in three people will experience at least one phase of insomnia at some point in their lives. But certain sleep habits can help. I recommend the following:

- Establish and maintain a consistent sleep schedule and routine. When possible, go to bed at about the same time each night and wake up at about the same time each morning. This kind of regularity helps many people fall asleep and wake up more easily.
- Plan to exercise earlier in the day. Vigorous exercise in the hours just before bedtime can interfere with sleep. Exercising in the morning, on the other hand, enhances alertness when you need it most—at the beginning of the day—and promotes better sleep at night.
- Set the stage. Adjust the room temperature; most people find that cooler (sixty to sixty-five degrees Fahrenheit) is better than warmer. Adjust the lighting—the darker, the better. An eye shade or room-darkening blinds are helpful for some people. If you tend to stir at the slightest sound, try using white noise to mask other sounds. A fan at low speed or an inexpensive white noise generator can serve this purpose. Alternatively, there are numerous CDs and downloadable MP3s featuring all types of natural soundtracks, atmospheric "soundscapes," and trancelike music, which can be quite

pleasant and relaxing. How about ninety minutes of chirping crickets? A rolling ocean? A distant thunderstorm?

- Avoid coffee and other sources of caffeine (including many types of tea and soft drinks, some brands of aspirin, and chocolate) after midmorning. The stimulating effect of caffeine can last for many hours and interfere with your ability to fall asleep at night. Caffeine is also a diuretic, which will increase urinary frequency.

- Limit alcohol use. Alcohol can disrupt brain electrical activity and undermine normal sleep architecture by suppressing the rapid eye movement stage of sleep.

- Avoid or limit naps. Napping can disrupt your natural sleep cycle and prevent you from feeling tired enough to fall asleep when you really want to—at night. If you must nap, make it a brief (thirty minutes or less) "power nap."

- Try drinking something hot, such as a cozy cup of chamomile tea or a glass of warm milk (preferably skim or 1 percent fat). Milk contains L-tryptophan, an amino acid that can help you relax.

- Don't try to force sleep if you're not tired; you'll set yourself up for tossing and turning. If you're still awake after twenty minutes or so, get out of bed and do something quiet and nonstimulating. Return to bed when you feel sleepy.

- Find your path to a relaxed state. For some people, ten minutes of reading or television will invite dozing. For others, the opposite is true. A warm bath, a massage, listening to sports radio—consider the many possibilities.

- Review your medications. Some over-the-counter drugs contain stimulants, such as caffeine or pseudoephedrine; a number of prescription medications can interfere with sleep as well. Review your medications with your doctor. Frequently, a simple change in your medication-taking schedule can solve the problem.

If your sleep problems persist, talk to your doctor. You might have a treatable underlying illness that's interfering with your sleep, such as obstructive sleep apnea or depression. Sleeping medications should be used as sparingly as possible and always under your doctor's guidance.

Learn Something New

In the MacArthur study, the characteristic that correlated most robustly with good cognitive functioning in aging was level of education. We think that education may help keep memory strong by inculcating the habits of being a lifelong learner—for example, reading a lot, becoming involved in intellectually challenging projects, and intensively exploring topics that you find fascinating.

Yaakov Stern and fellow researchers at Columbia University reported in 1994 that higher levels of educational and occupational attainment appeared to be related to a reduced risk of Alzheimer's disease. They speculated that higher education might be a proxy for *cognitive reserve*, a set of skills or repertoires that could serve to delay the onset of clinical symptoms. In this scenario, people with similar levels of underlying brain pathology would vary in terms of symptom severity, depending on their level of cognitive reserve. More recently, Stern hypothesized that cognitive reserve may be based on more efficient utilization of brain networks or the brain's ability to recruit alternate brain networks as needed, for example, in the context of injury or disease.

A separate series of brain imaging studies appears to support this hypothesis. Among Alzheimer's patients with similar levels of symptom severity, functional imaging with SPECT and PET scanning revealed that the brains of the people with the highest education levels showed weaker blood perfusion and metabolic activity than the brains of people with the lowest education levels. In other words, the brain of a more highly educated person had to exhibit a more profound degree of dysfunction than the brain of a less educated person in order to produce the same level of symptoms.

In a 2004 study, researchers at Rush University Medical Center in Chicago reported additional evidence in support of the connection between educational background and Alzheimer's disease symptoms. They examined the relationships among underlying Alzheimer's brain pathology at autopsy, years of education, and symptom severity in a group of elderly Catholic clergy who had been participants in a longitudinal study. Consistent with the Columbia group, they found that among people with similar levels of Alzheimer's disease pathology, those with higher levels of education exhibited fewer symptoms and better overall functioning.

The Columbia group and others have also reported that, once Alzheimer's disease is diagnosed, high levels of education correlate with more rapid decline than low levels of education. In other words, when the amount of brain pathology becomes severe, cognitive reserve can no longer hold off the symptoms and the decline is steep and swift.

The Rush researchers also found support for the idea that the critical factor in cognitive reserve is not necessarily years of formal education per se but rather ongoing participation in cognitively stimulating activities. In a community-based sample, they found that people who more regularly engaged in cognitively stimulating activity were less likely to come to a diagnosis of dementia; importantly, frequency of engaging in cognitively stimulating activity was more important than years of education in reducing the risk of incident Alzheimer's disease. Cognitive reserve therefore appears to be malleable and dynamic, resulting from a combination of innate factors (the genetic component of intelligence) and ongoing life experience (regular engagement in cognitively stimulating activities).

Regardless of your education level, you, too, can be a lifelong learner. You don't have to go back to school (although that would probably do wonders for your memory!). Less ambitious efforts can also be beneficial. You might learn how to play a musical instrument or take up an intellectually engaging hobby. As with physical exercise, I find that it helps to schedule time on most days for mental exercise. Reading regularly, keeping up with current

Memory Myth: I Never Finished College—Now I'm Afraid I'm More Likely to Have Memory Problems than Someone with an Advanced Degree

It's true that people with an advanced education appear at lower risk of memory disorders and age-related memory loss than people with less education. But we think that what's most important is not whether you earned a Ph.D. or a B.A. thirty years ago but rather whether you continue challenging yourself intellectually throughout life. Continuous learning is both a use-it-or-lose-it strategy for enriching your life today and an investment in the future—helping you build up a "cognitive reserve" of neuronal connections. This reserve will help keep your memory and other cognitive functions sharp, even in the face of age-related changes in the brain.

affairs, and playing challenging games that require strategic thinking are all good ways to exercise your mind. Here are some other ideas:

- Go to theaters and museums.
- Plan day trips, as well as longer vacations, to interesting destinations.
- Plan, research, and execute a do-it-yourself home-improvement project that requires creative design work.
- Design and plant a new garden.
- At work, initiate or volunteer for a project that involves a skill that you don't normally use.
- Delve into research on something that you've always been curious about.
- Explore the Internet. You can gain access to a wealth of information on any conceivable topic.
- Join a book group.

- Join a club to play chess, bridge, or poker.
- Take a course to learn a new skill that requires effort and practice, like playing a musical instrument, painting, or website design.
- Do puzzles and brainteasers. In addition to the crossword puzzle in your newspaper, consider using books, magazines, and the Internet to find math brainteasers and word problems. Jigsaw puzzles challenge the mind, too.

Moderate Alcohol Intake

Alcohol use can either harm or protect your memory, depending on how much you consume. There is no question that heavy drinking contributes to memory loss. Excessive alcohol consumption is toxic to neurons and is the leading risk factor for Korsakoff's syndrome, a disorder caused by thiamine deficiency and characterized by sudden and usually permanent memory loss. On the other hand, research suggests that moderate alcohol consumption (one or two drinks per day) may help prevent dementia.

If you have been drinking heavily, discontinuing or sharply reducing your alcohol consumption can help prevent further memory loss and may permit the restoration of whatever loss you have already suffered. If you do not drink, I wouldn't recommend that you start to do so. Your memory won't suffer if you avoid alcohol, especially if you follow the other measures for maintaining optimal memory.

Engage in Life!

What's your passion? What area of interest is so completely absorbing that it commands your full concentration? For some people, it's the visual arts, music, or theater. For others, it's religious devotion or political commitment. It can be athletics or science, nature conservancy or animal rights, child welfare or another humanitarian cause. The possibilities are virtually limitless. The particular object of your consuming interest is less important than the fact that you have something that gives your life a sense of purpose. The best of all worlds is to find a way in which your passion and interests can form a bridge to connect you to others in your family, your community, or the outside world.

What does this have to do with preventing memory loss? Plenty. First of all, having an abiding passion gives you the impetus to pursue new knowledge and learning. It can also induce you to connect with other people who share your interest. And having something that makes your life worthwhile can help guard against depression and act as a buffer against stress, two causes of memory difficulties. Finally, in a world that can all too easily make us feel insignificant, participating in something meaningful, particularly in a context of giving to others, helps to engender a sense of personal efficacy—the ability to have an effect and make a difference.

Manage Stress

It's difficult to concentrate when you're under severe stress, and poor attention is one of the main barriers to effectively encoding new memory. The physiological features of the fight-or-flight response interfere with mental focusing in the moment. Living with chronic significant stress can impair your memory over the long term; high levels of cortisol, a stress hormone, are harmful to the hippocampus. You can't control all the stressful events in your life, but you can control your reactions to them.

There's no magical stress buster that works for everyone. You need to find activities and coping strategies that are effective for you. For some people, the answer is yoga or a nature walk; for others, it might be listening to music or having a heart-to-heart conversation with a close friend. Exercise is a proven method of relieving stress. Aerobic exercise, such as running, brisk walking, bicycling, and swimming, is an excellent way of burning off stress and negative emotions. Resistance training (weight lifting) is an underappreciated form of exercise with excellent stress-relief effects.

Relaxation Techniques

It usually takes more than sheer willpower to achieve a state of inner calm when you're anxious or upset. That's where relaxation techniques can come in. These are methods of conditioning you to "dial down" the psychological and physiological components of the stress state. Most of these techniques are easy to learn, though some do require a bit of practice at first. Consulting briefly with a clinical psychologist or another practitioner with specific expertise in this area is often a good way to get started; alternatively, there are a number of well-produced instructional books and videos available.

- **The relaxation response.** This is a technique developed over time more than thirty years ago by Herbert Benson, a cardiologist at Harvard, as part of his effort to help patients combat the physiological underpinnings of hypertension and hypertensive heart disease. The relaxation response is intended to lower heart rate, blood pressure, and respiratory rate.

  In order to attain the relaxation response, sit quietly in a comfortable position, close your eyes, and relax your muscles, moving from your toes up to your face. Try to clear your mind of all thoughts by focusing exclusively on your breathing and repeating the word "One," either silently to yourself or softly aloud. If you find your attention drawn to a distracting thought or sound, refocus on "One" and your breathing. Practicing this technique for ten to twenty minutes each day will train you to reach a relaxed state more and more quickly. Dr. Benson's 1975 book *The Relaxation Response* is an excellent resource.

- **Progressive muscle relaxation.** Edmund Jacobson, a psychologist and physiologist who pioneered progressive muscle relaxation in the 1930s, believed that individuals could attain relaxation by appreciating the difference between tension and release in the muscles. While sitting comfortably or lying down, close your eyes and concentrate on major muscle groups in your body, starting with your feet and working your way up to your face. First, tense the muscles in your right foot by clenching your toes, holding the tension for ten seconds. Then quickly release the tension. Next, do the same thing with your lower right leg, followed by the entire right leg, and so on, working your way through all of the major muscle groups in your body. The idea is to experience the sensation of releasing physical tension. Edmund Jacobson's original 1938 book, *Progressive Relaxation*, provides a comprehensive overview and outlines the recommended sequence of muscle groups.

- **Visualization.** Find a quiet spot where you will not be disturbed, get comfortable, close your eyes, and visualize yourself in a place that you associate with ultimate relaxation, tranquility, and well-being; it might be a particular location that you've visited or a place you've seen in a photograph, or it can be a place entirely of your imagination. Concentrate on what each of your five senses would experience in this specific place—what you'd see, hear, feel, smell, and taste. Many people think of their favorite beach on a warm summer day, a gentle breeze, a rolling surf, salt spray, and seagulls. Others imagine themselves floating in a cool mountain lake, gazing up at fluffy clouds passing by. Or you might think of a favorite room from your childhood, surrounded by your prized possessions. After about five or ten minutes, mentally depart from this idyllic spot and gradually refocus your attention on your external surroundings.

- **Diaphragmatic breathing.** The goal here is to take progressively deeper breaths that move your diaphragm, the muscle between the abdomen and the chest. Lie down and inhale through your nose. As the air fills your lungs, let it push your abdomen up and out about an inch. Hold your breath for a second or two, then slowly exhale and let your abdomen fall. With each inhalation, imagine that you are breathing in relaxation; with each exhalation, imagine that you are breathing out tension and anxiety. Continue for five minutes or so.

167

Several relaxation techniques have been found effective for reducing stress. See the sidebar "Relaxation Techniques" for details of these methods.

Organize Your Thinking, Organize Your Life

All too often when people come to me with memory concerns, the underlying problem is not a neurological disorder but rather a shortcoming in their ability to get organized. Just as it's easier to find what you're looking for on a well-organized desk than on a messy one, it's easier to remember virtually anything when your day is organized than when it's chaotic. I will frequently recommend a pocket calendar or a PDA in which to record important information, including appointments, contact information, to-do lists, and so on. You'll find a full description of the organizational strategies and other techniques that I find indispensable in Chapter 10.

Routinely Take Precautions to Protect Your Brain

Whenever you engage in an activity that introduces the potential for head injury, use appropriate protective gear. Far and away, the most common cause of brain injury is a motor vehicle accident; failure to use a seat belt significantly increases the risk of serious injury. Participation in recreational sports and contact athletics also requires taking routine precautions. This means wearing a helmet when motorcycling, bicycling, in-line skating, rock climbing, hang gliding, and skiing. Helmets and mouth guards are essential for contact sports, such as football and ice hockey. A mouth guard reduces the risk of concussive injury in contact sports by deflecting forces from a blow to the chin or jaw that would otherwise reach the skull base. Mouth guards should also be used when playing soccer, basketball, and rugby or when engaging in martial arts, boxing, and wrestling.

Head trauma is a major cause of memory impairment in young people and a risk factor for later development of dementia. Taking routine precautions to protect your brain from injury is one of the surest ways to protect your memory.

Yes You Can! Maintain a Positive Attitude

Although you can't choose your parents or your genetic heritage, many factors that affect your memory are within your direct control. Your nutritional habits, physical activity level, depth of social engagement, extent of involvement in lifelong learning, degree of vigilance regarding prevention and management of health problems—these are among the many factors that shape your memory function, present and future. And you control each and every one of them. Don't dwell on the things you cannot control, and don't feel that you must make every change in your life all at once. Review the strategies outlined in this chapter, set realistic goals for yourself, and begin with one step . . . today.

The Next Step

This chapter reviewed thirteen strategies you can implement to prevent memory problems and achieve optimal memory. In the next chapter, I describe a variety of practical, tried-and-true behavioral techniques you can utilize to improve everyday memory.

CHAPTER 10

Practical Strategies to Enhance Everyday Memory

A variety of strategies have proven to be highly effective in helping people improve their memory for new information and skills. These strategies can be divided into organizational methods, effective learning behaviors, and memory techniques. I personally rely on many of them to help me put names to faces, remember what people tell me, avoid misplacing keys and other items, and retain complex information.

The memory–enhancing strategies described in this chapter are not difficult to master. Indeed, many are based on elementary principles of learning that you probably already use implicitly. But if you employ them more often and with greater awareness, you will find that previously frustrating forgetfulness will diminish, and you will gain a new measure of control over the tidal wave of information and memory demands that surge at you each day.

You can learn these strategies on your own by reading this chapter. If you're the type of person who benefits from added motivation or structure, you might consider attending a memory training course at a local medical center or arranging a series of individual consultations with a clinician who specializes in memory and other cognitive problems.

Get Organized

Organization is one of the bedrock concepts for improving everyday memory performance. Being organized is a matter of creating effective systems for routinely handling different types of information and everyday situations that require memory. Some organizational strategies can be created quickly and simply; you can designate a specific place for certain items right now. Other strategies require some up-front investment in time, energy, and thoughtful consideration. However, once an organizational system is in place and running smoothly, it assures you that important information will be durable and accessible. Most important, it frees up time and resources, allowing you to deploy your mental energy for more creative, productive, and gratifying purposes.

Manage Low-Contrast Information

Most people need to mentally access a multitude of information throughout the day—for example, telephone numbers, e-mail addresses, appointment dates, and items to be purchased before the weekend. This is what I call low-contrast information because it's inherently indistinct: most telephone numbers consist of a ten-digit sequence; all appointments are pegged to date, month, and year; and so on. The human brain was not particularly well designed to lug around all of this low-contrast information in an easily accessible manner, which is why in 1993, the personal digital assistant (PDA) came to be.

With the advent of the PDA, time-honored organizational tools, including the address book, desk calendar, note pad, and to-do list, morphed into a single, compact, portable device. PDAs allow the user to enter recurring events, such as monthly staff meetings or your nephew's birthday each year. You can link contact data to appointments, organize time-sensitive to-do lists, and take paperless notes. You can even synchronize your PDA with a computer database so that you can enter information at your keyboard and have a backup of all of your data. Many PDAs have wireless Internet capability, and most can be programmed to emit a sound to cue you to do something at a designated time.

I am a huge fan of the PDA because of its compact portability, programmability, and interactive features. Before you conclude that I own stock in one of the PDA manufacturers (I don't), let me say that the old-fashioned pen-and-paper method can also be effective for helping you remember everyday details. Whichever of these tools you select, high-tech or low-tech, the key is utilizing it consistently to record and organize your daily flow of low-contrast information.

Meetings and Appointments. Record your appointments and important dates in your PDA or pocket calendar and keep it with you at all times. If you don't use a PDA, use a notebook-style weekly calendar that has paper for writing down important information. Check in with your PDA or appointment book at regular times during the day, perhaps after each meal.

Daily Tasks. In addition to noting your appointments, keep a list of the miscellaneous things that you have to do each day or week: people to call, items you need to purchase, routine maintenance on your car or home, and so on. Keep these to-do lists in your PDA or notebook, and check them at regular intervals or at least at the start and end of each day.

Names, Addresses, and Phone Numbers. Keep your address book up to date with complete contact information for friends, family, and professionals or companies with whom you do business. All PDAs contain an address book function. If there is something specific that you want to remember about a particular person (for example, the names of his or her children), note this within your contact information. If you haven't seen or spoken with the person in a long time, referring to your note can serve as a cue to help sharpen your memory for important personal details.

Vital Information

Record vital information in your PDA or notebook. You may want to list the medications you take and when to take them, your medical history, names and phone numbers of your doctors and health insurance company, emergency procedures, your homeowner's insurance contact information, credit card information, and work and cellular numbers of your closest relatives and friends. Password protection of sensitive personal and financial information is always a good idea. Store important documents, such as insurance papers and medical records, in a logically organized and clearly tabbed file cabinet or other designated location. More sensitive information, such as passports, wills, original receipts for valuable possessions, and other primary financial information, should be kept in a fireproof home safe or bank safe deposit box.

Belongings

Just as you create a system for recording important information, you should also create a system for keeping track of personal items. Designate a specific place in your home for your most important personal belongings (keys, cell phone, glasses, wallet, handbag, laptop computer, and so on) and *always* put them there when you're not using them.

Checklists

For procedures that you use infrequently and may have trouble remembering (for example, using a digital camera, burning a CD, or initializing your home security system), write the steps down and keep them with the relevant equipment and product manuals. Create a backup file of these procedures in your computer.

Locations

Keep maps of your area and other places you visit regularly in your car or in a designated location at home. Before going somewhere new or unfamiliar, locate your destination and route on a map. There are a number of travel websites that provide printable turn-by-turn driving directions and include mileage. When you've established your route, visualize as much of it as possible before you set out.

Maintain a Clutter-Free Environment

Keeping your personal and work spaces uncluttered induces you to create systems for storage, which in turn helps you remember where things are. Minimizing clutter will minimize distraction and allow you to focus more intensively on what's in front of you, increasing the likelihood that you will absorb and retain new information.

Behaviors for Effective Learning and Memory

How well you retain new information isn't just a matter of how smart you are—it's also a matter of how smartly you approach that information. Maintaining focus and ensuring comprehension are critical "front-end" processes for effective encoding. Following are several ways that you can adjust your behavior to improve your ability to learn new information that you hear, read, and see and then commit it to memory.

Focus

Sustaining attentional focus and absorbing dense information at a high rate of speed become more difficult with age. In fact, the gist of one major theory of cognitive aging is that a slowdown in the speed of information processing is the fundamental cause of age-related memory loss. In this scenario, reduced processing capacity causes an informational bottleneck, which results in less information crossing the threshold from working memory into short-term storage. Nevertheless, there are steps you can take to improve the likelihood of absorbing and remembering information.

* When someone is talking to you, look at the person and listen closely. If you did not understand something that was said, don't be shy about asking the person to repeat it or to

speak more slowly; confidence in knowing will more than offset the embarrassment you may experience at the moment. The same applies to absorbing written material; rereading a difficult passage to ensure comprehension is usually preferable to forging ahead with partial information.

- If the information you are hearing is something you need to keep in mind in order to do something later (working memory), paraphrase what was said or incorporate it in a response. For example, if your friend says, "We can go to the Mexican restaurant on Main Street or the Chinese restaurant on Broadway," you might ask, "Do you prefer the Mexican place on Main or the Chinese restaurant on Broadway?"
- Minimize interruptions. If someone asks you something while you're in the middle of reading or working, ask if the person can wait until you're finished. Don't answer the phone until you've completed what you're doing; let your voice mail or answering machine take the call.

Repeat

Repetition helps you encode information by forcing you to pay attention to it. To more effectively remember factual information, repeat it, either out loud or to yourself. When you meet someone for the first time, try repeating the person's name by working it into the conversation. Immediately after someone gives you directions, repeat them to the person.

Ensure Comprehension

Understanding something is a prerequisite for remembering it. When you grasp a difficult concept or the internal logic of a complex mathematical system, you are at a tremendous advantage in remembering all of the associated minutiae that go along with it. Comprehension allows you to appreciate similarities between new material and old material; relating something new to something familiar enhances memory. Asking questions during a lecture is one way to check comprehension. Repeating newly learned material to another person induces you to organize it in your own thinking; teaching someone else a new concept forces you to become entirely comfortable and fluent with it yourself.

Make a Note

In addition to writing down addresses, phone numbers, and other information that you need on a regular basis, write down important things that you need to know even just once or occasionally. We all have the experience of having an important thought spontaneously come to mind while we're in the midst of activity. Perhaps you're driving to work and a new business idea occurs to you. Or it could be a question you want to ask your doctor at your checkup next week, an idea for your daughter's birthday present, a book you'd like to read, or restaurants you'd like to try. Don't assume that you will be able to recall the thought thirty minutes later when you're sitting at your desk; make a note as soon as you can. The purpose isn't simply to have a written reminder. The act of writing something down helps reinforce it in your memory— so much so that you might not need to refer to your notes to cue your recall.

Practice Spaced Rehearsal

Although you might assume that intensive exposure to new information (cramming) is the best way to learn something, research has taught us that this is not the case. Learning that is spread out over time (spaced rehearsal) is more durable than learning that is concentrated within a short period (massed trials). You will remember something more effectively if you rehearse it once a day for three days than if you rehearse it ten times in ten minutes.

Do the Little Things Now

Don't clog up your to-do list with little tasks that can be dispatched quickly. When a small request that requires a response lands on your desk, the time it takes to file it for future action plus the time you will spend getting back up to speed on it for a second time ends up being time wasted. Dispensing with a little job right away obviates the need to remember it later.

Be Patient

As I mentioned earlier, one of the main reasons that memory capacity declines with age is that the brain processes information more slowly. But just because it takes you longer to absorb something doesn't mean that you won't get it eventually. So be patient— give yourself time to understand new information.

One of the most inspiring findings of the MacArthur Foundation study was that many of the participants said that when mental pursuits were important to them, they could compensate for the slowdown in brain processing by being patient with themselves and working harder. There's a lesson here for the rest of us: perseverance helps keep the mind sharp.

Memory Techniques

These are tricks of the trade to help you with memorizing. Some are time-honored techniques that have gotten many students through high school, college, and beyond when they needed to memorize an enormous amount of information. They can help you improve your everyday memory.

Mnemonics

A mnemonic (the first *m* is silent), derived from Mnemosyne, the Greek goddess of memory, is a device used to assist memory. Chances are that when you were in school, you learned or devised several mnemonics to memorize specific information—things like "All Cows Eat Grass" for the notes that fall on the spaces of the bass-clef musical staff or "My Very Easy Method Just Set Up Nine Planets" for remembering the names of the planets in the solar system. Mnemonic devices are effective for remembering listlike information that you will use repeatedly over time. They may not be as practical for remembering a one-time shopping list; pen and paper work better for this.

Associations

When you learn something new, immediately relate it to something you already know. Making connections is essential for building long-term memories; it makes the information meaningful, thus improving the odds that the hippocampus will consolidate it. A convenient way to remember the name of someone you just met is to think of all the people you know with the same name.

Making associations is also an effective way to remember passwords or pin numbers that, for security reasons, you don't want to write down and carry with you. When you create your security codes, do this with an association in mind. You might consider making your password to a members-only professional website something that you can associate with your profession— for example, 057528 for the month and year and your age when you received your professional degree.

Chunking Information

Chunking is an organizational method of sorting a large group of items into subgroups on the basis of a common characteristic. Suppose I gave you the following list of twelve grocery items (and you happened not to have pen and paper handy): spring water, sponges, apples, dishwashing liquid, coffee, tangerines, lemonade, laundry detergent, grapes, milk, limes, paper towels. It would be difficult to remember twelve different items over the twenty minutes you needed to drive to the supermarket. By chunking them into three subgroups (fruit, beverages, household cleaning supplies), you make the information much more manageable because you've essentially reduced twelve items to three, using each subcategory as a cue for its four members.

Chunking can also be used to divide a large sequence of items into several shorter sequences. If you're again caught without pen and paper as someone is giving you a ten-digit phone number, rely on the usual three-three-four subgrouping of digits. The number 6178714902 is tough to recall; 617-871-4902 is easier.

Method of Loci

This technique was devised by the ancient Greeks and continues to be extremely useful for managing complex or lengthy material that you need to commit to memory, for example, giving a speech without notes or PowerPoint. Think of a highly familiar route, perhaps your commute to work or a favorite vacation destination. Now imagine traveling the route and note the series of landmarks you would pass along the way. For your speech, relate each main talking point to the succession of landmarks on your route.

As you speak, imagine traveling your route. Each landmark or locus will function as a cue to trigger your recall of associated information. You can use other familiar locations, such as the rooms in your house, as loci for this method. But you don't have to restrict yourself to physical locations; you can use other sign-posts in your life, such as the months of the year, your family members ordered chronologically by age, and so on. The concept remains the same: relate each idea or concept to a specific locus.

The SQ3R Method

SQ3R stands for Survey, Question, Read, Recite, and Review. This method is particularly useful for integrating and remembering a substantial quantity of information, for example, from a textbook or lengthy professional material you need to master.

Survey. The first step is to gain an overview of the material, via a quick read-through or skim. Reading chapter headings and sub-headings or the first sentence of each paragraph will yield a mental outline of the material. Look over all associated graphics, including figures, images, and diagrams. If the material contains a concluding summary and associated study questions, read them as well.

Question. The second step is to question yourself about what you've just read. Formulate your questions based on the main points you gleaned from your initial survey. Make the questions provocative and interesting; when you read the material fully in the next step, curiosity will galvanize your focus and your questions will prepare you to categorically encode what you read.

Read. Now carefully read the material for comprehension. Think about your questions as you read. Note taking and underlining should be minimal, focusing only on key concepts. Taking too many notes at this point can interrupt the flow of information and degrade your comprehension.

Recite. As I mentioned earlier, speaking aloud about what you've just read, either to yourself or to someone else, is an excellent means of checking your comprehension and deepening your understanding of the material. Take more detailed notes.

Review. Come back to the material a day or so later. Review any notes you made. Ask yourself how what you've read complements or contradicts other information on the subject. Finally, return to your questions from step two. How would you answer them now? What questions are you left with? Review the material briskly several more times over the course of the next week or weeks. As I discussed earlier, this type of spaced rehearsal will promote effective memory consolidation and retention.

Putting the Strategies into Practice

I've just reviewed a range of different approaches to enhance everyday memory. Do you need to use them all? That depends on what sorts of things you tend to have the most trouble remembering.

Some strategies tend to be universally effective; I would argue that everyone needs a PDA or a notebook to keep track of contact information and appointments. But most people will identify specific problem situations in their lives that are best remedied by customized solutions. Take a few moments to consider your daily routine and the recurring memory problem areas that make your life difficult, that siphon off disproportionate energy and focus. Imagine the time and energy you could liberate if you could devise a system that pushed back on these problems, reducing them to minor, routine tasks.

Once you have identified the areas where you need improvement, focus on the strategies that can make a positive difference. Or devise a novel solution of your own, utilizing the principles I've reviewed in this chapter. Some common memory troubleshooting strategies are summarized in Table 10.1.

TABLE 10.1 Troubleshooting Memory Problems: Common Memory Lapses and Strategies to Overcome Them

What You Forget	How to Remember Better
Names	When you meet someone for the first time, use his or her name in conversation
	Think about whether you like the name
	Think of people you know well who have the same name
	Associate the name with an image, if one comes to mind (for example, link the name Sandy with the image of a beach)
	Record the person's name in your memory notebook, personal organizer, or address book
Where you put things	Always put things you use regularly, such as keys and eyeglasses, in the same place
	For other objects, repeat aloud where you put them
	As you put an object down, make a point of looking at the place where you put it
	If you still don't think you'll remember, record in your memory notebook or personal organizer where you put the object
What people tell you	Ask someone to repeat what he or she just said
	Ask the person to speak slowly; that way, you'll be able to concentrate better

TABLE 10.1 Troubleshooting Memory Problems: Common Memory Lapses and Strategies to Overcome Them, *continued*

What You Forget	How to Remember Better
What people tell you, *continued*	Repeat to yourself what the person said and think about its meaning
	If the information is lengthy or complicated (such as advice from your doctor), use a small cassette recorder or take notes while the person is talking
Appointments	Record them in an appointment book, in a calendar that you look at daily, or in your personal organizer
Things you must do	Record them in your personal organizer or calendar
	Write yourself a note and leave it in a place where you'll see it (for instance, on the kitchen table or by the front door)
	Ask a friend or relative to remind you
	Leave an object associated with the task you must do in a prominent place at home (for example, if you want to order tickets to a play, leave a newspaper ad for the play near your telephone)
	If you must do something at a particular time (such as take medicine), set an alarm

Adapted with permission from Winifred Sachs, Ed.D., Center for Cognitive Remediation and Treatment, Beth Israel Deaconess Medical Center.

Professional Memory Training

Many people need nothing more than this book to learn and implement behavioral strategies and techniques to enhance everyday memory. These methods are also taught by clinicians in memory training seminars and in individual sessions. Several different types of specialists are involved in teaching memory enhancement techniques, including psychologists, speech pathologists, and occupational therapists.

Whether you need professional guidance in learning and applying these strategies depends on who you are and the specifics of your problem. Some people respond to the social interaction and support of a group-learning environment to get started and

Caveat Emptor

Beware of memory training programs that rely on a game-playing approach. There is no credible scientific evidence that simply playing games that require concentration or memory will allow you to transfer a benefit to the specific memory demands in your everyday life.

One type of memory game that purports to strengthen memory entails remembering the location of hidden items in a grid. Do you remember the 1960s TV quiz show "Concentration"? Parts to a puzzle were concealed within a grid consisting of thirty squares. Contestants had to solve the puzzle by remembering pairs of numbered squares that, when flipped over, would reveal partial information. Some computer-based memory training programs are based on this type of exercise. It's true that if you keep playing the same game, you will become more proficient at it over time. But remembering pairs of locations on a game board will not help you remember where you parked your car at the mall.

If you search the Internet for "memory training," you will come upon hundreds of websites guaranteeing a cure for your memory

maintain momentum. Others require the additional structure and motivation provided by individual consultation.

People whose memory problems are significant and are interfering with their ability to do their jobs and function in life tend to do best with a more intensive one-on-one approach that can rapidly address their unique needs. In a private consultation, a clinician can analyze the memory problem relatively quickly and design a customized program with a brisk feedback loop for fine-tuning. Whether you opt for a group or an individualized approach, choose one that is run by a reputable health professional. Working with an academically affiliated medical center or professional or with a clinician recommended by your doctor will increase the likelihood that you'll receive high-quality services.

problems. Many of these sites lead with a hard-sell pitch wrapped in pseudoscientific jargon. Some are predicated on a subliminal or hypnotic learning approach that promises that if you simply listen to the twenty-three-hour, eleven-CD set, various brain regions involved in memory will be magically activated.

One site promises "amazing instant results for a photographic memory," allowing you to memorize volumes of information in minutes. Another offers memory tools linked to the godhead and other divine sources. One of my all-time favorites is a program that awards the participant Olympic-style medals for various cognitive areas and includes a game of learning bird sounds as a tool for "mind expansion and building brain power." I must admit that the product pitch that began with "Lapses of memory can kill!" caught my attention.

What *does* work is a kit of practical tools that are designed to address specific memory problems, such as the strategies and techniques reviewed in this chapter and taught by qualified professionals.

Future Frontiers

No matter how good your memory is, you can always make it better by using the practical strategies described in this chapter. Effective attentional focus and organization will always be key assets for optimal memory; this will never change. What *will* change, however, is our ability to reverse degenerative disease processes, prevent memory disorders decades before they manifest, and augment normal cognitive and memory function through the use of cognitive enhancers. You will read about the frontier of memory research in the last chapter.

CHAPTER 11

On the Horizon

As I've discussed in previous chapters, there are many highly effective strategies for achieving and maintaining optimal memory. Staying active both mentally and physically and controlling health problems that can impair memory will help you prevent age-related memory loss. Cultivating memory-friendly habits through the use of organizational tools, such as a daily calendar or PDA, and practicing spaced rehearsal to retain complex material are tried-and-true ways to improve your ability to remember important information every single day.

By now you undoubtedly realize that Alzheimer's disease is far and away the most significant threat to memory in aging. Alzheimer's disease is the target of the majority of ongoing research into treatment and prevention of age-related memory loss and disease. We currently possess a range of therapeutic options for the symptomatic treatment of Alzheimer's disease and other memory disorders, and we are gaining knowledge about the biology of memory and neurological disease at an astonishing rate. The near frontier in memory research is the development of disease-modifying therapies aimed at halting and reversing neuronal damage. I reviewed some of the promising medications under development in Chapter 8, but more revolutionary methods for treatment and prevention are also on the horizon, albeit a more distant one.

Recent research on stem cells, unspecialized precursor cells with the capability to differentiate and proliferate, raises the prospect of curing neurological disorders, but it also presents a host of important ethical questions. Gene transfer methods are also in the very earliest stages of investigation. Another highly controversial area of research and clinical practice is cognitive enhancement—the use of therapies to expand the bounds of normal memory and other cognitive functions.

The current and potential future role of all of these therapies raises many questions for individual users, physicians, and our society as a whole. Is it ethically acceptable to devote financial and intellectual resources to making intelligent people more intelligent or to engineer super memory capacity? Is it ethically acceptable to withhold this capability when it is within our grasp? Who should pay for this? Who decides which individuals should gain this advantage? What type of society do we want to have?

Preventing and Curing Memory Disorders

There are currently no FDA-approved uses for gene therapy or stem cell methods in the treatment of memory disorders; all of the work in these areas is at the early investigational stage. However, research in the realm of cell transplants and gene therapy may hold the promise of preventing or curing memory disorders, such as Alzheimer's disease. These technologies may one day be used to prevent age-related memory loss as well.

Some experimental paradigms involve a combination of cell transplants and gene transfer methods. In some cases, cell transplants are being used as vehicles for ferrying genes into the brain and other parts of the body for therapeutic purposes. In other experiments, cells are genetically modified before implantation to make them act in a specific, potentially therapeutic way.

Gene Transfer

Gene transfer methods were initially thought of as having the greatest potential benefit in the treatment of diseases caused by a single genetic flaw, such as Huntington's disease or sickle cell anemia. Multifactorial diseases, such as Alzheimer's, are not ideal targets for gene transfer methods because they are caused by a profoundly complex interplay among multiple genes and environmental factors. However, scientists are experimenting with a variety of ways to treat neurodegenerative disorders by using genetically altered tissues to effect repair or enhance function in areas of the brain that are important for memory.

Brain disorders pose special problems for standard gene transfer techniques. Although most gene transfer methods utilize a harmless, neutralized virus as a vector, or delivery system, for transporting genetic material into targeted cells, viral vectors are typically too large to pass through the natural protection of the blood-brain barrier in order to reach target areas in the brain. Alternative transfer methods for targets in the brain are being investigated, including direct injection and the use of liposomes (fatty spheres) as transport vehicles.

Researchers at the University of California, San Diego, developed a method of genetically modifying skin cells to express *nerve growth factor* (NGF), a protein that helps neurons survive by repairing damage and stimulating their regeneration. Beginning in 2001, modified skin cells taken from eight patients with mild Alzheimer's disease were implanted into brain structures in which cholinergic cells are typically destroyed by Alzheimer's disease.

Researchers reported in 2004 that the surgery was successfully completed in six patients and appeared safe and well tolerated. Two of the eight patients had complications during the injection, leading to a modification of the original procedure. PET scans showed increased metabolic activity in areas of the brain with the implants compared with activity in the brains of similar patients without implanted cells, suggesting that NGF had produced a positive physiological effect. In addition, the annual rate of cognitive decline was reduced by 40 to 50 percent in the implanted patients, which is significantly better than the typical response to currently available medications. Ceregene, the company sponsoring this research, plans for further clinical trials on genetically modified skin cell implants at Rush University Medical Center in Chicago.

Genetic methods might one day prevent memory problems altogether and endow us with superior memories. One potential target for genetic modification is the NMDA receptor, a neuronal docking point for specific neurotransmitters involved in learning and memory. In 1999 scientists at Princeton University, the Massachusetts Institute of Technology, and Washington University reported on research in which they were able to produce a genetically altered strain of "smart" mice with extra NMDA receptors. In experiments, these mice learned and remembered better than their genetically "normal" counterparts.

Scientific concerns are significant, associated with the unforeseen future impact of gene transfer on the human genome. In fact, one gene transfer clinical trial was stopped after a child developed leukemia, possibly as the result of a genetic mutation caused by an unanticipated interaction between the therapeutic genetic material and other genes. The future success of gene transfer methods depends in part on refining techniques for precise delivery of genes to targets, thereby preventing unintended genetic interactions.

One day, it may be possible to use gene therapy to enhance memory and other cognitive functions in people who are healthy. Profound ethical issues arise when we consider the implications of genetically enhancing normal individuals or selectively engineering desirable characteristics in humans. Compelling arguments can be made on either side of this issue.

Stem Cell Transplants

The discovery that the mature human brain possesses neuronal stem cells that yield new neurons into advanced age was groundbreaking and has provided major impetus to research into the potential of stem cells to definitively treat degenerative disorders, including Alzheimer's disease. Researchers hope that stem cells might be able to restore damaged brain functions by replacing cells that were destroyed. Stem cells might also be able to slow or stop further damage by helping to bathe neurons in protective chemicals that the stem cells themselves transport and express. Most experiments involve transplanting stem cells directly into the brain through imaging-guided needle injection, but some researchers are using intravenous infusions of stem cells mixed with a drug that can cross the blood-brain barrier.

When neuronal stem cells have been implanted into the brains of animals and humans, they have taken root, so to speak, proliferating and connecting to preexisting neurons. In one experiment, laboratory-grown human neuronal stem cells were transplanted into the brains of aged rats, resulting in improved performance in an experimental learning paradigm. The old rats were able to learn and remember a route through a water maze as well as their younger counterparts. These findings are encouraging. They offer hope that stem cells might one day be able to repair brain damage from trauma, stroke, or other brain diseases.

Preliminary findings on the use of stem cells in treating the depletion of dopamine-producing cells in Parkinson's disease have produced mixed results. Clinical trials here and abroad have found the stem cell implants significantly improved symptoms in some patients—to the point where they no longer needed dopaminergic therapy; however, the symptoms worsened in other patients. As with any type of organ transplant or tissue graft, one of the major obstacles to overcome with stem cell transplants is to prevent a rejection response in which the body's natural immune defense attacks the new cells.

Early experiments with neural stem cell transplants have yielded a wealth of basic information about stem cells and the work that needs to be done before stem cell transplantation can become a viable therapy. To be effective, the transplanted cells need to be rendered specific to the task at hand. If the therapy calls for an increase in dopamine, for example—as in Parkinson's disease—then stem cells capable of becoming dopaminergic neurons must be used.

Unfortunately, stem cells don't come to the laboratory presorted. The challenge here is to find a way to separate out the specific stem cells that are needed from all the others in a batch or to genetically manipulate stem cells to make them develop into the desired cell type. Another challenge is to develop a reliable way to produce these cells in sufficient quantity for treatment.

Stem cell research has generated controversy because the primary sources of stem cells are discarded fertilized eggs from in vitro fertilization procedures and aborted fetuses. After federal funding support was restricted to a small subset of cell lines that had been in existence prior to September 2001, research continued to be funded privately. In November 2004, Californians voted in favor of a $3 billion initiative to support stem cell development and research; other states are likely to follow. Private institutions, including Harvard, have created funding and infrastructure in support of this work.

Alternative methods of producing stem cells are also being developed, including using tissue from neonatal umbilical cords. The use of adult stem cells is also a major focus of research.

The Search for an Alzheimer's Disease Marker

In order to prevent Alzheimer's disease, we must first be able to identify at-risk individuals either before or very early in the preclinical phase, the period during which disease activity (deposition of beta-amyloid) is occurring but has not yet reached a level sufficient to produce clinical symptoms.

We do not currently have a true preclinical marker for early identification of the vast majority of people who are destined to develop Alzheimer's disease; development of early detection strategies is a major focus of research. Although Alzheimer's susceptibility genes, such as ApoE, offer partial information on risk, additional tools will be needed, including brain imaging studies, blood tests or other biochemical assays, and more sensitive neuropsychological testing than we have today. Ultimately, early detection of Alzheimer's disease will probably be based on some combination of these methods.

Although stem cells from adults do not possess the perfect plasticity of embryonic stem cells—that is, the potential to become any cell type in the human body—methods are being developed to coax a greater range of specialized cell types out of adult stem cells. Another line of research is focusing on drugs that can stimulate the brain to grow its own new stem cells.

Cognitive Enhancers

Imagine that you're on a tight deadline with a project that demands your full concentration. What if you could take a pill that would enhance your ability to stay on task and remember minute details? You can.

Cognitive enhancers—medications to augment the function of the normal brain—are not the wave of the future. They are here, obtainable today to anyone with a credit card and an Internet connection. Their easy availability poses serious safety risks to individuals who use them without medical supervision, though. I caution against taking any of these medications on your own.

We possess the knowledge and the tools to fundamentally alter our internal milieu: our ability to focus our attention in the service of memory; control our sleep and wakefulness; modify our inclination toward social engagement versus hostility or withdrawal; promote or diminish libido and sexual performance; amplify, mute, or otherwise modulate the emotions we experience.

Medications approved for the treatment of brain disorders including Alzheimer's disease, multiple sclerosis, and attention deficit–hyperactivity disorder are beginning to be prescribed off-label to healthy people who are seeking a competitive edge. Several studies have evaluated the effectiveness of some of the Alzheimer's drugs in middle-aged people with normal memory function and found that the people performed better on cognitive tests, as I discussed in Chapter 8. But this is only the beginning.

Researchers are investigating whether existing medications can affect the physiological underpinnings of normal cognitive function to improve attention, concentration, working memory, consolidation, and long-term memory. In addition to cholinesterase inhibitors used in the symptomatic treatment of Alzheimer's disease, medications under study include methylphenidate (used for attention deficit–hyperactivity disorder) and modafinil (a stimulant prescribed for narcolepsy and several other neurological conditions).

Another avenue of cognitive enhancement that is under study is the use of medications that can alter memory for emotional events. We can disrupt memory consolidation through the use of beta-blockers, a type of blood pressure medication. Research is being done with victims of severe psychological trauma to determine if use of these drugs can reduce the risk of developing posttraumatic stress disorder.

But what about using these drugs to eliminate a mildly traumatic memory, such as a job loss or the breakup of a romantic relationship? Or a vaguely annoying experience, such as a slight from a coworker? If we eradicated depression and anxiety in the same way that polio was eliminated, would our society suffer a loss in artistic sensibility? Or emotional attachment and bonding?

The interest in cognitive enhancers is so strong that I have no doubt that they will come into more common use in the years ahead. But the existence of drugs that can extend the capacity of normal cognitive function raises a host of ethical and philosophical questions. Clearly, taking a pill to help you think better is different from laser refractive surgery to improve vision or plastic surgery to enhance physical appearance.

Martha Farah and Anjan Chatterjee at the University of Pennsylvania have written recent excellent reviews regarding the ethical dilemmas posed to individuals, physicians, and society by the forthcoming proliferation of cognitive enhancers. They raise issues regarding the erosion of character and the mutation of personal identity. If we believe that struggling with adversity helps build character, then might not the elimination of adversity result in a downgrading of our societal strength, a lack of grit and forbearance? Aren't pain and emotional struggle essential aspects of being fully human?

What about availability and distribution? Would it be fair to expect the health insurance system to cover the cost for cognitive enhancers? If the answer is no, then only those able to afford them would reap the benefit, widening the gap between the haves and have–nots.

If a colleague at work were using cognitive performance–enhancing drugs, would you feel compelled to follow suit in order to maintain competitive parity and be in position to gain the advantages of superior performance in the form of promotion and remuneration? Would your employer have the right to expect you to use cognitive enhancers in order to be more productive or effective as an employee? What if there was evidence that use of enhancers decreased the risk of making serious errors, as in the case of an airline pilot or a medical resident in the twenty-third hour of a shift?

Optimal Memory Redefined

We are living in an interesting time. The very fact that we now face these ethical and existential questions is reflective of just how far we have come in our understanding of how memory works and our prospects for improving it. We may soon have the tools to eradicate memory disorders and turn back the clock on age-related memory loss. With these tools in hand, we will have the potential to expand the boundaries of optimal memory.

Additional Resources

Organizations

Alzheimer's Association
225 N. Michigan Avenue, 17th Floor
Chicago, IL 60601
800-272-3900 or 312-335-8700
alz.org
e-mail: info@alz.org

This nonprofit organization supports research on treatments for Alzheimer's disease and provides information and support to families. The association has about two hundred local chapters.

Alzheimer's Disease Education and Referral Center
800-438-4380
alzheimers.org

This site, associated with the National Institute on Aging, offers comprehensive information on Alzheimer's disease and a link to clinical trials.

ClinicalTrials.gov
clinicaltrials.gov

This is an Internet portal, sponsored by the National Institutes of Health, leading to comprehensive information on clinical trials for all diseases.

Dana Foundation
745 Fifth Avenue, Suite 900
New York, NY 10151
212-223-4040
dana.org
e-mail: danainfo@dana.org

The Dana Foundation, which finances neurological and other health research, is a nonprofit organization of more than two hundred scientists dedicated to advancing education about brain research.

Harvard Center for Neurodegeneration
and Repair
Goldenson Building Room 524
Harvard Medical School
220 Longwood Avenue
Boston, MA 02115
617-432-3370
hcnr.med.harvard.edu

Launched in 2001, the HCNR is a decentralized community of Harvard Medical School neuroscientists and neurology research-ers working in the medical school and eight affiliated teaching hospitals. The HCNR supports the movement of basic discover-ies in the field of neurodegenerative disease from the bench, through basic research, and on to clinical trials. The mission of the HCNR is to speed the process by which relevant discoveries reach the patient population.

InteliHealth
intelihealth.com

This website features consumer health information and research news from Harvard Medical School as well as other top health care organizations, including the National Institutes of Health.

John D. and Catherine T. MacArthur Foundation
macfound.org

This organization, which supported the landmark MacArthur Foundation Study of Aging in America, finances research on the brain and other subjects. You can search for the most recent studies at this website.

National Institute of Mental Health
6001 Executive Boulevard
Bethesda, MD 20892
866-615-6464 or 301-443-4513
nimh.nih.gov
e-mail: nimhinfo@nih.gov

This National Institutes of Health branch is a source of information on depression, anxiety, and other mental illnesses.

National Institute of Neurological Disorders and Stroke
NIH Neurological Institute
P.O. Box 5801
Bethesda, MD 20824
800-352-9424 or 301-496-5751
ninds.nih.gov

Another branch of the National Institutes of Health, this institute provides information about Alzheimer's disease, stroke, and other neurological disorders, including the latest findings on drug treatments.

National Institute on Aging
Building 31, Room 5C27
31 Center Drive, MSC 2292
Bethesda, MD 20892
301-496-4000
nia.nih.gov

This branch of the National Institutes of Health posts information on its website about the latest research on aging and age-related health conditions.

Books

Eat, Drink, and Be Healthy: The Harvard Medical School Guide to Healthy Eating
Walter C. Willett. New York: Simon & Schuster, 2001.

An authoritative resource on the foods and nutrients that can increase or decrease the risk of health problems, written by the chairman of the Department of Nutrition at the Harvard School of Public Health.

Keep Your Brain Young: The Complete Guide to Physical and Emotional Health and Longevity
Guy M. McKhann and Marilyn S. Albert. Hoboken, NJ: John Wiley & Sons, 2002.

This book covers the full spectrum of concerns about aging and the brain, from everyday problems with memory loss, nutrition, and mood to potentially devastating illnesses, such as Alzheimer's disease and stroke.

Memory Fitness: A Guide for Successful Aging
Gilles O. Einstein and Mark A. McDaniel. New Haven, CT: Yale University Press, 2004.

Written by two psychology professors, this book describes how memory works and changes with age. It presents memorization strategies, a review of medications, and information about Alzheimer's disease, including advice for caregivers.

*The Seven Sins of Memory: How the Mind Forgets
and Remembers*
Daniel L. Schacter. New York: Houghton Mifflin, 2002.

Drawing on the latest findings from imaging studies of the brain, a professor of psychology at Harvard University offers a clear, compelling discussion of the types of memory lapses that people experience and why they happen.

Index